Table of Contents

AUTHENTICITY
Living with Meaning and Purpose

MICHAEL HARDIMAN Ph.D.

Contents:

Chapter 1.
Authentic Self Worth

"The most uncouth of our afflictions is to despise our being"

Montaigne

Introduction

Self-worth is a central strand in the cable of a healthy and fulfilled life. The concepts of self-worth and self-esteem are the gold standard of popular self-psychology, and rightly so. Discovering that how people see and feel about themselves has dramatic and long-term effects on their quality of life is one of the great contributions of self-psychology. That said, there is a great deal of delusion about what self-worth actually means, and, in addition, a great deal of misinformation of what it takes to develop the healthy balanced relationship with the self.

Most current writings on self-development hold the assumption that you are important. There is broad acceptance that it is good for you to take care of yourself. There is a wide acceptance that good self-esteem is an aspiration worthy of endeavour. These are the core values that underlie almost all schools of counselling, therapy, human resources management and personal development training. These values could be considered a key driving force behind the enormous cultural and social development in over the past half century. Attitudes to child development, parenthood and education are all deeply affected by these values. The importance of the individual and his or her happiness has become the currency of modern self-help literature. As sociologist Weintraub summarises, "In our age, more than any other we are captivated by an uncanny sense that each of us constitutes an irreplaceable human form and we perceive a noble life task in the cultivation of our individuality, our ineffable self. Thus, the importance of self-worth as a key element in happiness comes on the tail of a great social change that led to the development of individuality as a fundamental value.

Defining Self Worth

Human beings are the only creatures on the planet that develop a relationship with themselves. It is worth taking a moment to reflect on this phenomenon. That relationship is at work every day you are conscious, and often in the background of your day to day activities. The relationship is formed as we develop our cognitive abilities from early childhood into adulthood. Therefore, ones' early formative experiences strongly influence the way your relationship with yourself works. This relationship will stay with you throughout your life, it is the only relationship you will never lose, and will profoundly influence your happiness.

One of the particular periods in childhood that are important is what is called by psychoanalyst Jacques Lacan 'the mirror stage'. This is the stage when it becomes obvious to the onlooker that a child recognises itself in the mirror. To do so requires an awareness of oneself as a person. This self-awareness continues to grow in complexity throughout the formative stages of life. Alongside this self-awareness there is a parallel process of developing an attitude, sometimes out of conscious awareness, to that self. This occurs through a psychological process called introjection.

Introjection is the process by which a human being internalises the messages from significant others and believes and feels those attitudes to himself or herself. Thus, for example, a child who is constantly criticised for being awkward, giddy, in the way, not good in school (or any mix of these and other perceived defects) can grow into someone who feels stupid, slow, unwanted and so on and so forth. In other words, they come to believe that they are a defective person. Conversely, the well-loved child, who is consistently exposed to encouragement and affectionate care develops a sense of self-worth that is positive and life enhancing. And then again there is the 'spoiled child' whose every whim is indulged, lacks discipline and impulse control, becomes demanding and difficult, and develops an unrealistically positive view of their capabilities. They develop what is termed unearned high self-esteem.

By the time a person comes into their early adult life they will have built a resilient set of attitudes and beliefs about themselves. This is called their self-concept. Part of that self-concept is their level of self-worth. That self-worth is carried into adulthood and strongly affects the individual's decisions, achievements, relationships and personal fulfilment

Healthy Self-Worth.

When an individual has received consistent positive, realistic and caring treatment during childhood and adolescence he or she is highly likely to develop a positive and healthy sense of self-worth. This means that they consider themselves to be a person of value, who, to a large extent, accepts themselves, even those aspects that are problematic. They tend to accept their limitations and are not embittered towards themselves when they find flaws. They are secure in themselves and establish good boundaries whereby they do not let others take advantage or mistreat them. Equally, they are able to let others around them be themselves, not needing to control others or overly seek attention and approval. They can comfortably give and receive love. They are also likely to have a healthy sense of danger, and do not engage in high levels of risk taking for its own sake. They may, for example, enjoy the challenge of risky activities such as wind surfing, or mountaineering. Even though there is danger attached to these and similar activities, the danger is not the reason for engaging in the activity. In essence, people with healthy self-worth have introjected positive and valuing messages from their surroundings during their formative years. Almost all forms of counselling/therapy try to cultivate and nourish this kind of self-worth in an individual. It is a crucial ingredient/element in living an empowered and fulfilling life.

Unhealthy self-worth

Problems with self-worth can be divided into two categories. On one hand, there is unwarranted and unrealistic high self-worth, and on the other negative depreciating low self-worth. The former is better known as narcissism. Narcissistic people regularly mistreat others around them. Alternately, those with low self-worth are particularly vulnerable to abuse and mistreatment at the hands of others. More specifically they are easily led into damaging relationships with the polar opposites, narcissists. It is important therefore to describe this form of dysfunction. The description of narcissism below is given with the specific goal of helping the reader understand this dysfunction and therefore be better able to deal with it when it is encountered.

Narcissism

The term 'Narcissist' comes from ancient mythology. The function of myth making in ancient cultures was to help people make sense of life. These stories are timeless because they carry moral insights into the various struggles and flaws that inhere in human nature. The myth of Narcissus is one case in point and is particularly relevant to the present discussion of self-worth. In the classical myth Narcissus was a hunter who was renowned for both his beauty as well as his scorn for those who loved him. Nemesis, the goddess of divine retribution, seeing this flaw led Narcissus to a clear pool where he could see his reflection plainly. He so fell in love with himself that he lost all other interest and eventually wasted away and died.

The important element in this myth for the current discussion lies in the fate of Narcissus. He wasted away. People who are filled with self-aggrandisement and snobbery also waste away. Their lives are ultimately empty. Part of this emptiness occurs because they are unable to partake in some of the most nourishing and enriching experiences open to a human being; the main one being that of intimacy. Narcissists are incapable of intimacy. To experience the enrichment of the soul by opening and meeting the soul of another is impossible for a narcissistic person. This is because all their interactions with others are focussed on using the other person for their own ends. These ends include attention seeking, using others resources to enhance their own position in ways that support their vanity, this can include using others for status, for financial gain, for security.

They also fail to grow spiritually. By this I mean being able to experience the self-transcendent conditions of deep love, appreciation of beauty, being transported by the sense of connection to a higher being, or higher power through music, prayer or engagement with nature.

Narcissistic people are also likely to be destructive of others. They are prone to what is called narcissistic rage, which is provoked by anything that is perceived as a threat to their sense of self-importance. Narcissists use others while at the same time being incapable of empathy. Empathy is that human capacity for understanding at a cognitive and emotional level the experience of others, to see and feel the world from another's viewpoint. Empathy is an essential aspect of any close human bond.

Psychologists Twenge and Campbell write in their book "The Narcissism Epidemic" that: " In fact, narcissism causes almost all of the things that Americans hoped high self-esteem would prevent, including aggression, materialism, lack of caring for others, and shallow values. In trying to build a society that celebrates high self-esteem, self-expression, and "loving yourself," Americans have inadvertently created more narcissists — and a culture that brings out the narcissistic behaviour in all of us. This book chronicles American culture's journey from self-admiration, which seemed so good, to the corrosive narcissism that threatens to infect us all." Thus, not all the efforts to help people develop high self-worth are successful. Bloated egos, self-absorbed and grandiose sense of entitlement are not markers for emotional health. Rather they are the opposite of healthy self-esteem that is grounded in reality, takes account of the rights of others and is based on a realistic care and respect for oneself.

Most aspects of human dysfunction can be found along a range from mild to severe. With narcissism, the individual may reflect the 'common or garden' variety: being described as a bit full of themselves, to the extreme of an utterly self-absorbed, vain, parasitic and intimidating bully. Woe betides those who engage in a significant relationship with such an individual. It leads to emotional exhaustion, desperate despair, loss and sometimes actual physical danger.

Low Self Esteem.

The second form of dysfunction is that of low self-esteem. It is an affliction that causes great difficulty for those caught up in its web. It refers to a negative and diminishing relationship with oneself. Several notable characteristics are reflected in this problem.

A lack of confidence.

Low self-worth leads people to lack realistic levels of confidence in their abilities, in the realms of work, learning/education, relationships and a lot else. The reader will note the use of the word 'realistic' in the above sentence. Realistic means that which relates to reality. Low self-worth does not mean having no confidence in doing something you are no good at, that's called sanity! Rather low self-worth means that an individual is over critical, judgemental and negative in areas where they do have ability and potential. As a result, fearing failure and all the pain that it brings to an already shaky heart, they will often no longer try. In doing so, they diminish their experience of life and fulfil their own prophecy of failure. They are, in essence, disempowered by virtue of a negative and critical attitude to their abilities and potentials.

Over Compensation.

A second feature that may result from low self-worth shows itself when an individual builds their need for self-worth compulsively around only one aspect of their ability. The internal belief driving this problem is that if they succeed at this one aspect of life they can then feel good about themselves.

Classic examples of this abound in the world of workaholics. Some people are driven into ill health and addiction as a result of compulsively focusing on proving their worth in one dimension of being. Common examples are; career success, material wealth, sexual conquest, exhausted caring for others and so on. None of these activities in themselves are negative. They can be seen the outworking of low self-worth when they grow to a level of destruction that dominates a life to the exclusion of others healthy aspects of living

Tolerance for Mistreatment.

Perhaps one of the most common and insidious expressions of low self-worth is the acceptance and tolerance of mistreatment by others. Here again the myth of Narcissus can help. In addition to Narcissus being condemned to waste away while gazing at his own image, he is accompanied by Echo, a wood nymph who has fallen desperately in love with him. Echo has fallen foul of the goddess Hera who punished her because of her incessant chattering. Her punishment is that she can only repeat the words of others, and therefore has no voice of her own. (giving us the modern use of the word echo). This part of the story is useful as a picture of someone who loves a narcissist. The love is unrequited, the person loses their voice which represents their identity. They are completely limited to the narcissists voice-identity, and eventually fade away into oblivion. Anyone who has witnessed the long-term effects of people entrapped in such a relationship can attest to this phenomenon.

A key to understanding how people become lost in such relationships is the effect of low self-worth. Self-worth refers to the value a person places on their personhood and on their life. We naturally protect and cherish the things we value. When I set out to buy a used car, I like to meet someone who places great value on their car. When I buy it from them, I know the car will have had a full-service record. It will be clean, well taken care of, with few if any dents and scratches etc. I will enjoy the quality condition as I drive away, bringing the unfortunate machine into a different world of neglect and mistreatment. I have no interest in my car, don't care if it gets rusty, untidy, and unkempt. I have no value on it except to get me from A to B for a period of time until I try to sell it on to someone like me who has an equal level of disinterest in it. (otherwise they wouldn't buy it!) A general rule of thumb is that we do not treat well what we do not value, nor do we mind so much if someone else does not treat well what we do not value.

If a person does not value, or undervalues their life and personhood, then they are likely to accept and tolerate mistreatment at the hand of others. They can find themselves being taken advantage of in all aspects of their lives. Their partners can treat them with contempt, use their resources as they need, refuse to cherish or care for them is a way that supports and encourages their happiness. Their children can grow up to diminish them, take what they want and equally neglect to give anything back. They can be bullied at work, overlooked when it comes to advancement and promotion, given the most difficult of tasks and so on and so forth. Low self-worth is a leading cause of this kind of dysfunctional living. A client of mine summarised it thus: "if treat yourself like a doormat, other people will walk on you"

Tolerance for suffering.

Closely related to a high tolerance for mistreatment is a high tolerance for suffering. Being mistreated is a specific form of suffering. There are others. Being stuck in menial or unsatisfying job is one. A person with low self-worth, as we discussed above, may not know the potential they have for advancement, or more positive change. Allied with an acceptance of suffering they can lock themselves into decades of unfulfilling working life that further diminishes them, because they believe that they do not deserve any better. They know they can cope with the chronic dissatisfaction and as a result do not take action to escape.

Lack of self-care and care for one's health can also be a result of low self-worth that, in turn, can lead to physical suffering. Physical pain is an alarm system in the body that tells us something is wrong. Low self-worth can lead to neglect the warning to get a proper check-up, because, for example, the cost of a visit to the doctor considered too much (the internal voice says, you are not worth investing in). By the time an appointment is made the delay may cause whatever disease entity to take hold often leading to much more serious condition and even death.

Depression

The topic of depression is a vast and complex terrain. It would require the remainder of this book to fully explore all the different aspects and theories as to the nature and cure for this common and terrible human affliction. Here I want to dwell on two aspects of how self-worth and depression are related: negative thinking, and unresolved loss.

One of the features of depression is a negative and pessimistic thought life. This usually takes the form of an internal dialogue which speaks just below consciousness about all the events and engagements with the world. Thus, the list of internal comments is characterised by critical, embittered and diminishing self-statements. Examples are: 'There you go again messing it up'. 'Of course, she's not interested in you, he/she much too pretty/successful/intelligent'. 'Don't bother applying for the course/job, you won't get it anyway'. 'You got a good grade/promotion/smile because they don't really know how stupid/ incompetent/ you are'...and so on and so forth.

The above are a small set of the kind of internal dialogues that can occur with low self-worth. Each of these barely conscious comments have the same emotional effects as if they were said by another. They hurt. In the case of an external agent you can argue back, disagree or simply refuse to listen. When they are within the mind, they are much more difficult to deal with but have the effect of creating a helpless and despairing orientation in life. One of the most well-known approaches to depression was developed in the 1970's by psychologist Martin Seligman who discovered the phenomenon of learned helplessness. In his research he found that if human beings find themselves in difficult circumstances over which they have no power to change, some will develop a hopeless/helpless attitude to their lives. When circumstances change to allow them to alter their difficult circumstances, they do not change this internal way of framing events and thus do not make any efforts to change even when they have the power to do so. In consequence they miss or avoid opportunities that could improve their lives. Thus, the pessimistic outlook leads to its own fulfilment.

A second strand in depression is almost always the presence of unresolved grief. Sigmund Freud understood depression in these terms because he saw a parallel between the normal and common characteristics of a grieving person and those suffering with depression. Grief is a healthy, temporary and intense emotional process that is given to us in order to help us to cope with the loss of people and things we love. It includes numbness, sadness, longing, pining, anger and the like. We see and accept these experiences in people who are bereaved in some shape or form. The intensity of the grief is strongly related to the level of loss. Thus, the loss of a child is recognised as causing the most intense form of sometimes hysterical and often inconsolable grief. Loss of a spouse, loved one, cherished pet and so on all bring different levels of grief commensurate with the intensity of the emotional attachment.

Depression also brings with it many features of grief except that there is no clearly identifiable loss to which these feelings are attached. Often, within the process of counselling, people who suffer depression do discover that there is, in fact, some unresolved loss of which they have been unaware. In the context of self-worth this is an important finding. People with low self-worth can and do experience depression as a direct result of the loss of self-love that is at the root of their relationship with themselves.

Anxiety

Low self-worth can also lead to a high level of anxiety. It is a truism that levels of anxiety are significantly related to the intensity of a threat. Thus, fear levels are very high if the danger level is high. People who suffer low self-esteem are already in a vulnerable state. They feel ashamed of themselves and feel less than adequate in life. This makes them very sensitive to criticism or failure from the outside world. The self is already fragile and any negative response from another further hurts this fragility. As a result, there is a feeling of fearfulness in everyday life, particularly when engaging in any activity that risks the judgement and/or requires the approval of others. This fearfulness is a form of anxiety.

Building healthy Self Esteem

The foregoing discussion briefly examined the importance of healthy self-esteem to living a fulfilling life of your own making. How to enhance this part of the self is however another matter. Before doing so I want to dispute much of what is written in the self-help world on this topic because I believe it leads to greater difficulty, and causes more problems than it solves. One of the fictions that inheres much of the human potential/self-help industry is that everybody has vast potential and everyone is extraordinary. The good news is that this is not true and that you don't have to be either extraordinary or brilliant to have a fulfilling life. In the wider scheme of things each individual life is somewhat insignificant. Look around you. Look at all the people milling around in life trying to survive, to stay alive, to carve out a modicum of happiness. Think about rush hour in the tube stations in London. Millions of individuals running hither and yon to get home, to meet their lovers, to collect their children, exhausted by evening only to repeat it all, day after day. Think about it. How many of us are extraordinary? Very few.

That prophetic philosopher Frederic Nietzsche did much to challenge the illusion of personal greatness. He shows us that in every era of human history very few people embodied either genius or greatness. He considered the rest of us to be what he termed the "bungled and the botched". I don't accept the derision he holds for ordinary unexceptional people but I believe he is right in exposing the fallacy of personal greatness for most of us.

We would do well to ignore most of the delusional encouragement meted out by the more 'new age' oriented section of the self-help industry. Rather than buy into the fiction of personal greatness we need to have a realistic perception of who we are, warts and all. We are no less in need of love and respect by being ordinary. To suggest otherwise is to build a basis for self-worth on some delusional beliefs about ourselves, a belief that will ultimately be exposed by life experiences, and then lead to a sense of deep despair. Buying into a fictional view of one's own greatness leads for most (except for those few that are actually great/exceptional or those afflicted by pathological conditions such as narcissism) to a sense of despair and guilt.

World athletics competitions provide us with a good example of how we can better understand human potential. These athletes work constantly at their craft. They hone and prune their bodies and minds, preparing for that brief moment in the sun when their ability will be tested. The standards are incredibly high. The pressure is enormous. The gun goes off and they run/swim/jump for their pride, destiny, family, country or a mix of all these and other values. What I am certain of is that only a tiny percentage of us could do what they do, even if given all the training and dedication. They are bright stars in the firmament of graceful strength and speed.

On the reverse side of this coin we can learn something by watching reality TV talent shows such as the X factor. Here we can witness delusion at work. We can witness a tone deaf and musically crippled person audition for a place on the world stage. We can laugh at the judge's reaction, their incredulousness that the person really believes that they can sing, or that they have talent. Good singing involves several closely related factors, a person's ear: that is their ability to hear music appreciatively, and their voice which carries a melody in key, and their rhythm which allows them to follow the natural rules that is part of the structure of music. Someone who has a good ear but no voice would never present themselves for such a competition. That is because they know they cannot sing. They can hear it. The unfortunate ones who provide the audience with most laughter are those who have no ear for music and no voice. Thus, they cannot know that they sound awful. Of these then there are two sub groups: those who will take the advice of those around them, and those who don't. Every now and then one of these tone-deaf, vocally challenged people has been encouraged by family members (who share the same musical handicaps) to audition for stardom. They provide the darker aspect of the show by finding themselves humiliated in front of millions. One of the judges rather cynically commented to a contestant: "just because you won a rosette at a donkey derby doesn't mean you can run in the Grand National".

Then, from out of all those unfortunately deluded, and talentless contestants (some who show great confidence, and high unearned self-esteem) steps a shy, modest, nervous youngster who opens his/her mouth and you are stopped in your tracks. Even in such a mundane reality TV show sparkles of great talent can show themselves. If greatness is elusive and most of us do not have a giant within us to awaken, what then is the basis for taking your own life seriously and valuing yourself? It is based on the fact that you are very important in a limited way by virtue of being a person. Philosopher Martin Heidegger's formulation and the philosophy of existentialism that grew from his influence, explains that each human being is a unique expression of human existence. People come into life, grow into themselves, express themselves in the world and then die, most often having produced offspring. So, let us continue in this line to discover if there is some element that can help us to ground a value for our lives, other than simply that one is alive.

Your worth lies firstly in your identity as a unique human being. This is what I call the 'divine spark', that expression of humanity that is as Victor Frankl tells is unique in both essence and existence and thus is neither expendable or replaceable. And secondly in the possibility that how you live will in some small way (for most of us) influence the tapestry that is the human condition. This view is acceptable to both religious and non-religious positions alike. In a religious world view this is the way God created us. We are responsible for whom we become and ultimately all our acts, both constructive and/or destructive, good or evil, are significant. Our behaviour changes us, and affects the world including the rest of the human race. In a non- religious world view, we inhabit this planet and how each of us acts will, to some extent, determine how long we last here. If we destroy the earth we will die, if we destroy each other we will live in fear and turmoil. If we respect and cherish ourselves and each other we will benefit. Thus, we can bridge the gap between the promotion of individuality on one hand and the task of social responsibility on the other.

Building a healthy loving and respectful relationship with oneself is part of this process. To learn to love and respect oneself is a process that very often has a decision at its core. If, as a result of painful and damaging formative experiences you have developed feelings of shame and inadequacy about yourself, then you have a choice to continue to support and nourish that negative and deprecating relationship, or you can change it. I understand that this appears very simplistic, in fact it is simple, but it's not easy. The spiritual commitment to turn around on the path and change direction always occurs at a single point, and yet it is only the start of a journey. Similarly, changing your relationship with yourself, from one of negativity and criticism into one of support and encouragement is also a decision. Once it has been made and you come to that point of commitment to changing the way you view and treat yourself then there are several useful tools to help along the way. These are summarised below.

Dismantling the Enemy Within.

Most people who suffer with low self-worth have internalised a sub persona that talks to them in their thought life. This "voice" is usually a metaphorical representation of some parental or authority figure from early life. This persona is sometime called the inner critic. I like to call it 'the enemy within'. Its role is very rarely to help you to improve. It disguises its criticism as some kind of constructive criticism when in fact, for the most part, its role is to diminish and destroy all the good, spontaneous and positive efforts at life by constant fault finding and ridicule.

One of the keys to dismantling this very powerful intrapsychic agency is to get to know it, and to understand that it is not you. Separating yourself from the voice can be helped along by firstly giving the persona a name. By doing so you immediately distance yourself from it. It now has a separate identity that you can engage with. Here is a useful metaphor. Imagine meeting an old acquaintance from school days. You sit down to have coffee and he/she begins to make a series of comments about you. He/she continues to find a whole plethora of negative things to say about you. At this point you can do one of three things (legally!) You can get up and leave. You can dispute the comments and reject them. Or you can bow down underneath the tirade and let it damage you. This scenario reflects what it is like to have an internal voice full of negativity and hostility beating you up psychologically. And similarly, once you have given it a separate identify you can begin to dismantle its power. Giving it a name is a first step in that process.

A second step is to write down the familiar themes of its criticism. By writing down the list of the common accusations you stop the internal rant and you get an opportunity to address the complaints.

Like all criticisms there are probably some elements of truth in them. By writing them down you get a chance to evaluate their importance. Some flaws can be dealt with through a simple process of acceptance. You do not need to be perfect to be worthy of love and respect. There is no perfection in human life. Others criticisms can be addressed by considering action to improve oneself. That is the best anyone can do. In all cases these criticisms can also be balanced by a recognition of other aspects of the self where positive characteristics and achievements can be acknowledged. Writing a list of these alongside the complaints of the inner voice can indeed be helpful.

Re-parenting oneself

Closely related to the above is the concept of re-parenting oneself. Most people have some notion of what it is to be a loving and healthy parent. In spite of this "knowing" some people, because of their own dysfunction may struggle greatly to do it. They may not have the emotional stability, interest or dedication to be good parents. They would however be able to tell you what good parenting involves. In a strange way we are all parents to ourselves. There is an intrapsychic agent called your 'inner parent'. This (metaphorical) agent can be harnessed to help build healthy self-worth by repairing the wounds of the past that have damaged your relationship with yourself. The central responsibility and role of a parent is to provide sufficient love, care, guidance and resources to a child in such a way as that child can grow into young adulthood capable of living a productive and enjoyable life.

Re-parenting yourself is a process by which you take charge of yourself with the intention of better care and respect. I like philosopher of religion John Hick's description of the values that drive good parenthood. He says "I think it is clear that a parent who loves his children, and wants them to be the best human beings they are capable of becoming, does not treat pleasure as the sole and supreme value. Certainly we seek pleasure for our children and take great delight in obtaining it for them; but we do not desire for them unalloyed pleasure at the expense of their growth in such even greater values as moral integrity, unselfishness, compassion, courage, humour, reverence for the truth and perhaps above all the capacity for love....to most parents it seems more important to try to foster quality and strength of character in their children than fill their lives at all times with the utmost possible degree of pleasure" Thus when we take the role of parenting our own lives, we do so with the intention of helping ourselves to grow into all that we can be. Gradually, step by step, by making consistent movement toward becoming a fulfilled and mature human being, as distinct from the self-absorbed trivial and shallow pursuit of instant gratification, often recommended by the worst elements of the self-help movement.

Designing a self-care program

Self-care is not selfishness. We have seen above that the simple pursuit of pleasure is not sufficient as a model of love for self. Self-care refers to a set of activities that promote healthy growth and development in body and mind. We have also seen above that people who are afflicted with low self-worth are inclined to live life with little or no proper care for themselves. In general, a self-care program will involve treating oneself with respect and behaving in ways that promote fulfilment and happiness. When faced with any decision a useful rule of thumb here is to regularly ask the question, "If I love and respect myself in this situation, what will I do"?

Another useful guide is to take the five senses through which all experience ultimately comes, and parcel out a set of tasks into each.

Sight-

Reading materials that bring enjoyment and stimulation. Watching movies that encourage and challenge. Looking at nature and beauty and allowing the experience to feed the soul. Wearing clothes and colours that suit us giving us a more positive feeling about the body.

Hearing.

At the present moment our world is traumatised by terrible wars in Ukraine and in the Middle East. Our own society here in Ireland is bedevilled by widespread homelessness and failures in the medical system leading to severe overcrowding in hospitals and long waiting list for medical care. Now almost every news bulletin and every Vox- pop radio program relays a stream of negativity and pessimism. We only need to hear so much of this to stay informed, the rest can only further depress and lead to despair. A far better option is to listen to music that soothes the soul and reminds of beauty and spiritual depth or the kind that creates excitement and joy. Going to classes/courses that challenge, stimulate and inform helps develop the mind, or to add new skills and creativity to the self.

Even more important is to choose to leave or avoid conversations that are negative or and critical of yourself or others. Sometimes we need to put up with a little constructive criticism where appropriate. This can happen in an otherwise positive and friendly loving relationship. Stay away from people who have nothing good to say to you, or continually find fault with everything around them.

Touch.

Human touch is an essential aspect of emotional health. Giving and receiving affection, enjoying sex, indulging in warm baths, sensual massage, sport, swimming, jacuzzi and the like are all ways to nourish this aspect of the self. A slightly more indirect aspect of touch is that of tactile experience. This occurs when our bodies are stimulated by our environment. The feeling of a warm breeze, or a powerful wind as we walk on the sea shore, or a country lane are good examples. Sometimes it is a matter of awareness, that is making a decision to 'tune into' the sensual experience as it is happening. You can walk along the seashore worried about life and miss the actual sensual experience of the walk. The exercise itself is helpful but will be all the more beneficial if you allow the fullness of the experience into consciousness.

Smell-

This includes using aromatherapy, essential oils, flowers in the home, becoming aware of the scents of new mown hay, perfumes, and the like. Finding scents that feel good and using them in everyday life can uplift and bring sweetness and pleasure.

Taste-.

Savouring your food, and trying new tastes. Living in the experience of enjoying the sensual experience of food and drink Eating slowly and discovering the subtleties of flavour and texture is both a lovely habit to practice as well as much healthier for your digestion.

At first glance these suggestions seem almost trivial and superficial but ironically it is their very simplicity that makes them so achievable. Taking time to invest in these and engaging in activities that are specifically suited to your own personality will have the effect of healing and rebuilding your self-esteem.

Worthwhile Activity

Our self-esteem is learned through experience. This means it can change. One of the strongest influences in how our self-esteem has been built occurs through the feedback to us from our early environment. It is thus hugely important to find and pursue activities that affirm our worth either through positive responses from others or through a sense of achievement. On their own these activities will not break the cycle of negative self-treatment, but they are one aspect of recovery. The kinds of activities that are most likely to benefit the task of rebuilding self-esteem are fundamentally connected to the kind of person you are and these are examined in detail in other sections of this book.

Avoid Toxic People

Toxic people are those who infect others with negative and destructive feelings and attitudes. They have been so damaged in their own lives that they cannot celebrate or value the worth and dignity of others. One particular group of toxic people are those that use others to affirm their own brokenness. I know it is very harsh to use this label because many who have suffered greatly do deserve our compassion and sympathy. However, this type of toxic person is more likely to be one who has experienced opportunities to rebuild a better life and failed to do so. They may have had a lot of people who have shown love and concern for them. The refusal to allow these influences to heal and rebuild means that they have invested themselves in being pitied. They have developed a victim syndrome, preferring the sympathy of others rather than the challenge to grow beyond the hurts of their history. The long-term effect is to create a bitter and negative view of life. And thus, they will automatically try to drag all that's good and positive down into the soup of bitterness from which they sup. A short exposure to such people will leave you feeling diminished, angry and frustrated. The other category of toxic people includes those described earlier as narcissists. Their toxicity consists of their willingness to use and abuse the sensitivities and needs of others for their own gain. There are many resources online that treat of this issue and if you believe that you are entangled with a narcissistic person it is essential to use these resources to help get you out of the situation.

Feed the White Dog

Often mistakenly attributed to Native American oral tradition, the story of the two dogs, one white and one black is a useful metaphor for how our inner thought life affects our self-worth. Evangelist Billy Graham gives the best version of the story. "An Inuit fisherman came to town every Saturday afternoon. He always brought his two dogs with him. One was white and the other was black. He had taught them to fight on command. Every Saturday afternoon in the town square the people would gather and these two dogs would fight and the fisherman would take bets. On one Saturday the black dog would win; another Saturday, the white dog would win - but the fisherman always won! His friends began to ask him how he did it. He said, "I starve one and feed the other. The one I feed always wins because he is stronger." Feeding the black dog means allowing the negative self-criticism to flourish. Rebuilding self-esteem means nurturing and promoting thoughts and behaviours that reassure you of your dignity and worth. It does NOT mean telling yourself lies about how brilliant and special you are. The key to healthy self-worth lies in the relationship between your view of yourself and reality. This is most important when exploring your abilities, talents and life purpose. I will examine these in more detail in a later chapter.

All the above relates to the challenge of overcoming low self-worth. However, the other side of the coin presents a different challenge and one that is more difficult to resolve. Unearned high self-esteem, and narcissistic attitudes and behaviours are a lot more difficult to address because there is no immediate relief, or pleasure gained in pursuing practices that address this problem. Ironically, self-help/therapy and popular psychology, with all its best intentions have provided some people, who already have the problem of a too high sense of self-importance with beliefs and practices that make the problem worse. These are those of the more recent entitled generation who lack resilience, tolerance for adversity, and hold unrealistic expectations of how life should treat them. To deal with this problem the kind of exercises that are requires involve deepening awareness of the suffering of others, practicing humility and learning empathy. The kind of affirmations required here would include ones that remind one of the brevity of life, the importance of love, the recognition of one's finitude and responsibility. The quote from theologian John Hick above provides a really useful set of values to pursue in undoing the toxicity that goes with overvaluing oneself and devaluing others. Philosopher Philip Rieff's criticism of the therapy world is useful here when he tells us that the cultivation of the self, taken as an ideal, is no guarantee against stagnation and despair.

Summary.

Healthy self-worth is a key ingredient in the overall project of a healthy fulfilling and empowered life. It is not simply the pursuit of pleasure for its own sake which often results in a constricted and ultimately shallow form of living. Healthy self-worth can be greatly facilitated by defeating the enemy within of the negative inner critic, re-parenting through a commitment to treat oneself with respect and care, and finally to pursue a self-care program through activities that affirm what is good and beautiful in life and challenge you to grow into the best you can be. Some might argue that one needs to have high self-worth in order to carry out these plans. To that argument I would say that there is a parallel here with those who struggle with the unhealthy condition of obesity. A healthy diet is something an overweight person must pursue in order to get to a healthier weight. Low self-worth is an unhealthy condition usually brought about by damaging experiences in early life. It can be changed by changing the psychological diet on which it is based. The wonderful thing about being human is that we do not have to be prisoners of our past. The power of freedom gives us the capacity to replace a lot of losses and to change the path set out for us at earlier times. Before turning to the topic of freedom, we must first examine what it means to be a unique self. This is the subject of the next chapter.

Chapter 2.
Authentic Selfhood

"The tragedy of life is not death but what we let die inside of us while we live"
Anthony De Mello.

Introduction

A client of mine recently made a comment about how he now finds himself in his life. He said "I just realised that I have never felt that I am behind the steering wheel of my life. The truck is moving along but in a direction that I never really wanted". In this short phrase he captured what is for many people the experience of living the dance of life to the tune chosen by others. That is the lot of many, and historically it was the lot of most. They lived and died using their productive energy to obey the rules, fulfil the roles, and meet the expectations and demands of others, without ever given thought to the possibility of creating a life of their own design.

As discussed earlier the primary emphasis in most of our history was on society creating a person to fit into its requirements, and very survival itself was often the goal. In pursuit of this task the family and educational systems worked on moulding people. This was achieved by the use of punishment and rewards designed to mould the individual into becoming what was needed by the adult world. The end result of this process is that by the time a person reached adulthood he has constructed a self that responds to the demands of the world.

This constructed self is often so powerful that sometimes the individual has to break down in some catastrophic way before they become free of it. For others, their whole life is lived out as a constructed self. They live and die without ever living their own life. Anthony DeMello comments in this regard that if, on your deathbed, someone else's life flashes before your eyes, then you'll know you got it wrong! Others come to realize that the life they are living is not fulfilling and is simply one designed for them by others and they have the courage and the awareness to do something about it. For most of us, to create our own life means getting to know our constructed self.

How does the constructed self work?

A constructed self is developed in response to the demands and expectations of the society into which we are born. The primary representatives of that world are your parents, your family and your educators. (A more detailed description of how we are shaped by such influences can be found in another of my books entitled "Misled? How Ideology can Capture your Mind."): These generally reflect the wider community in terms of what is considered appropriate and successful. This does not mean that your parents who engage in moulding, or your teachers (or at least some of them) did not have your interests at heart. It does mean that for the most part they did not realize that they were moulding you to fit a construction that has been handed down to them. They too were moulded by their adult world. On and on each generation shaping the young to fit a compliant, self-sacrificing, conforming model of what it means to be a person. Gradually honing and pruning the character, chipping away at too much self-confidence, or individuality, or self-expression. The adult world prepares the child to become an adult who will surrender the self for the better of the tribe/community.

As if to copper fasten this point I read recently in the local newspaper a full colour page advertisement for a course on "Purpose in Life". This course seems to rely heavily on the bestseller "The Purpose Driven Life" by Mega Church Evangelical Pastor Rick Warren. It seems worthwhile to reprint the text for it reflects clearly the philosophy that has shaped us for centuries. The course organiser writes: "You are not an accident. Even before the universe was created, God had you in mind, and he planned you for his purposes. These purposes will extend far beyond the few years you will spend on earth. You were made to last forever. The search for purpose has puzzled people for thousands of years. That's because we typically begin at the wrong starting point—ourselves. We ask self-centred questions like, what do I want to be? What should I do with my life? What are my goals? My ambitions? My dreams, for my future? But focusing on ourselves will never reveal our life's purpose. The bible says "It is God who directs the lives of his creatures, everyone's life is in his power" (Job:10) Self-help books often suggest that you try to discover the meaning and purpose of your life by looking within yourself, but Rick Warren says that it is the wrong place to start. You must begin with God, your creator and his reasons for creating you. The bible says self-help is no help at all. Self-sacrifice is the way. "My way to finding yourself, your true self." (Matthew 16.25.)

This account of our life purpose is no longer accepted by the majority of people in Western Europe, but its demise is recent and for centuries it held sway. It remains a powerful presence in other cultures and in certain regions in the United States. Clearly, in this vision of our lives, we are made by God for a purpose and our task is to discover what we were made for, and to follow that path. Most importantly we must not use 'ourselves' as the reference point for understanding our purpose in life. Rather, the guide for our life purpose lies outside the self. Someone or something else is the author of the script for our life. This form of thinking has, in fact, predominated the history of the human race. From Plato's "Republic" to Huxley's "Brave New World" we see the theme of creating and moulding people to actualize an ideal world. A Christian god that demands self-sacrifice as the central value is not that different from an emperor who demands complete submission, or a tribal community that requires complete submersion of the self for the good of the community.

In this view of the world you are neither significant nor worthwhile in and of yourself. That is the central tenet of all of this. You are to be moulded, or created for the use or purpose of God or community. And this moulding begins in childhood. The tools that are used in moulding you into whatever is required are the selective use of valuing and love. We know that two of our fundamental needs in early life are (i) a sense of belonging or attachment, and (ii) a sense of competence or value. We come into the world with powerful radar for these essential nourishing experiences. And we will do almost anything to get them.

As a parent gazes into the eyes of his/her baby, the love is generally instinctual and at this point unconditional. Gradually, however, the loving smile begins to take on a different tone. It is evoked more easily by certain behaviours on the part of the child, slowly but surely the child learns that to be a certain way is acceptable and lovable and to be another way is not. This is how we are trained. It is called socialisation.

Similarly, your value as a person becomes connected to how well you succeed at the kinds of tasks that are important for the wellbeing of the community. A simple example is found in the general way that boys and girls and treated differently. Young boys were encouraged to be successful at competition, to win and often to push the boundaries of physical achievement and to engage in risky behaviour. Conversely, they were (and to a lesser extent still are) expected to suppress certain emotions particularly one that display vulnerability: "big boys don't cry". Expressions of vulnerability are often met with, at best, a gentle disapproval and, at worst, severe ridicule. Words like "sissy", "pussy" and "wimp" are all part of our language to be used as forms of punishment for boys and men who show 'too much' vulnerability.

Young girls were praised for helping and caring and cooperating, for showing compassion and for suppressing emotions that reflect power: "good girls don't fight". I can recall the respect I had for a girl who walked into our all-boys school every day for the honours maths class. Her school did not have such a class as it was considered that girls didn't need to be good at higher level math. It is only in recent decades that women who married in Irish society were not forced to give up their careers. Looking back I realise that this girl's parents must have had a lot of courage to take on the system and insist on this education for their very bright young daughter; namely: Having a worthwhile career These are very basic examples of the way that socialisation works and barely capture the sophisticated and complex way that we are taught how to define ourselves in the world. Depending on the degree and extent that these practices are brought to bear will determine the degree to which we emerge into adulthood as a construction that may bear little resemblance to our real selves. It can be said that in some situations people live out their whole lives without ever reflecting on why that are living the way they are.

Anita arrives for a counselling session. She is friendly, refined, and deeply sad. Her eyes speak of a deep sense of loss. She is here she says because she feels empty and trapped. She describes herself as feeling that her life is just a constant effort, with no sense of joy or fulfilment. As the session progresses, I see a person of extraordinary sensitivity. She appears almost ethereal. I sense that something has happened in her life that resulted in her having to almost leave some vital part of herself behind and hide it in some secret place in the hope that someday she might be able to return and reclaim it.

She speaks of a childhood almost bereft of gentleness or warmth. Her intense interest and attraction to colour and form was brutally rejected as 'just so much nonsense'. Her talent and immediate passion for art was swiftly replaced by an insistence that science was the way she should go. And she did. In order to fit the demands of her parents and some of her teachers, she put away her love of art and trained her mind into the rigour of scientific endeavour. Now, very successful, she is a key member of a laboratory team dealing with sophisticated medical advances. Anita has become someone who is contributing to the tribe. Her intellect and energy provide skill that will help the tribe to survive. She is helping in the advances of medicine which we know adds to the treatment and care of people's bodies. All the 'Anitas' of this world added together make up a key part of our ongoing survival and flourishing.

Anita's story presents the distress that is the result of being forced to fulfil some role that may have little to offer in terms of our own nature or fulfilment. This is not just a matter of simply being in the wrong job. The forces brought to bear on her meant that she had to bury a part of herself. The love of form and colour, the passion for art are expressions of some aspect of her core self. These are characteristics of a person, not just a set of artistic skills. Had she been a more naturally scientific person, she would have suffered far less. Some of us are very fortunate in that the role we are socialised into fits naturally to the kind of person we are. Thus, not all the shaping and moulding process ends in pain. The naturally athletic young man enjoys that grace and skill of the game, and to the victor goes the spoils. The poor unfortunate chubby, short-sighted cerebral young man drags himself off to the dressing rooms with a sense of relief that his ordeal is over. And, of course, his sense of his own value in the world is damaged.

From our earliest consciousness of the world, which is preverbal and inarticulate, we have observed what we need to become in order to feel valued and loved. Just as the plant turns to the sun, so we as children learn subtle and not so subtle ways to grasp hold of this essential nurturance so that we can survive. We learn that certain behaviours get us attention, others are devalued. The gradual process of moulding our identities through the use of attachment and praise on one hand, or rejection and punishment on the other, leads most of us to construct a self for the purposes of this world. In general, this constructed self becomes our identity in the world. We live out our lives through it.

To some extent we all construct a self. What is important is to realize that this construction can reflect our true nature, or it may not. Thus, fulfilment comes only when we live, to a large extent, a life that is reflective of our true self. This is what is meant be 'authentic selfhood'. If we have constructed a self that does not reflect our true self then we will experience our lives as fundamentally troubled. Some may argue that there is no such thing as a true self. That everything is learned and constructed. To those I would say you have not spent much time observing children. From their earliest years, children begin to show a unique personality. If the adult world into which the child has been born recognises that the duty and responsibility of adults is to witness the emergence of that unique human being, to nourish its individuality and to encourage its unique expression, then that person will most likely grow up expressing their own unique life in the world. Responsible stewardship towards the emergence of the child into adulthood is not simply a matter of letting them do what they like. This is the straw man that some critics of self- development make. It takes far more attention, commitment and love to engage in relationships with our children that helps them become their unique selves.

Understanding Your Constructed Self.

The workings of the constructed self often involve an absence of self-knowledge and self-acceptance and a lack of a sense of worth and value. The relationship to the self is torn at the foundation. The individual has not incorporated into his or her life a deep sense of self-respect and a commitment to self-care (this has nothing to do with selfishness). The constructed self is the provisional life. A life lived in a compulsive search for a sense of value that is bestowed by others. Because nothing that is ever accomplished in this way will actually provide this, the individual ends up endlessly trying. Psychiatrist James Masterson is eloquent on this point when he says "A life ruled by the false self 's defence against inner emptiness ends up truly empty. However, it is far from empty of pain, suffering, depression, guilt feelings and elaborate schemes to deny one's own best interests. Many patients describe themselves, their thoughts and feelings as "numb". They trudge through daily tasks as if drugged, unable to find anything but a looming void at the centre of their lives"

A friend of mine once described an experience that nicely illustrates this point. He bought a young Springer spaniel bitch that was a bit highly strung. The dog had a habit of jumping up at the back door in anticipation that at some point the master would open it. Every now and then of course he would open the door and let the dog in. She would get into a frenzy of excitement as she felt the love and care he had for her. The next day of course he had to go to work. All day the dog tried the door, day in and day out. Every now and then the creature experienced the joy of his master's early return from work. And yet the animal's need was never filled. My friend related this story to me because he felt it very much reflected his own life: A driven compulsive search to find a sense of inner peace and acceptance, which he had mistakenly believed was in the hands of others. This can be juxtaposed with the true self in operation. We know that we have reached a high point of authenticity when we can say, "I am worthwhile and valuable in myself because I am expressing my true self in this life".

Those who are fortunate enough in their formative years to have people who are keenly attentive to witness the emergence of that person into adulthood, and who consistently find ways to encourage that unique selfhood, will suffer little conflict between their real self and their constructed self. In time, the experience of belonging, and attachment as well as the sense of competence and value become internalized. They can build a relationship with themselves based on these experiences. This process of internalising the relationship from significant others into our psyche becomes the template for how we relate to ourselves in our adulthood. Our relationship with ourselves, a unique aspect of being human, has profound effects on our quality of life as adults. Those who internalise a loving and respectful attitude become are comfortable with themselves and value their abilities and achievements. On the other hand, those who internalise a judgemental critical and rejecting attitude are awkward and critical of themselves, or as someone described it as "uncomfortable inside their own skin". In some cases, the internalised relationship can be so damaged that it leads to profound self-hatred. In this situation, that individual is quite likely to accept tremendous disrespect and even abuse from others. In the alternative they can dump their internal distress onto others, becoming critical, bullying and abusive.

For many of us the process of valuing ourselves is very conditional and we can value and love ourselves only if we are successfully living out as a construction defined by others. Many philosophers have paid attention to this problem. Probably best known in this regard are the renowned philosophers Martin Heidegger, and Jean Paul Sartre. These two explored the challenge it is to live a life that reflects a true self. Heidegger spoke of inauthenticity, living life that conforms to the dictates of the social but anonymous "They": living what he called a "they self". Sartre speaks of living in "bad faith": by failing to express oneself truly, usually out of fear of rejection or of failure. Jewish Philosopher and Holocaust survivor Elie Wiesel explains "when we die and go to heaven, and we meet our Maker, our Maker is not going to say to us "Why didn't you become a Messiah? Why didn't you discover the cure for such and such? The only thing we are going to be asked at that precious moment is "why didn't you become you"?

Thus, the endpoint in all this discussion is the challenge to live a life that reflects your true self. How do we do this? The answer to this essential question has two aspects. Firstly, it requires an awareness of what it means to have a true self, and secondly, it requires the freedom to become that person. Both these issues are large and complex and can be combined in the concept of what has been called self-actualisation.

Self Actualisation.

"Self-actualisation" is a term coined by Abraham Maslow and popularised by humanistic psychologist Carl Rogers. It became a central element in a movement in psychology best referred to as self-psychology. This movement has had a dramatic effect on popular thinking and on the institutions of modern society. Attitudes to child development, parenthood and education, counselling, therapy, human resource management, and religion are all deeply affected by the notion of self-actualisation. Abraham Maslow, one of the founding fathers of self-psychology is best known for tabulating that very impressive "hierarchy of needs". In his formulation he places self-actualisation at the top of the hierarchy. He understands that the most self-actualised person is someone who authentically lives their true self and has many peak experiences during their life. Much of the ideology of the self that appeared in that rosy time of the late 60's and early 70's can now be seen as naive and overly optimistic. I call this view of the self as the flower theory of the person.

Essentially the idea holds that if the human self (flower) is given the nourishment it needs, namely love and attention, praise and discipline, then it will flourish into a thing of beauty. Furthermore, this ideology was born in society that for the most part (at that time) was economically wealthy, and did not experience on its own soil the horrors of the two World Wars. Even the humiliation of Vietnam, was, to some extent, distant from the general populace. The sixties had been marked out by radical rejection of all things conservative, a celebration of free love, assisted by the use of drugs that fostered altered states of consciousness. Timothy Leary, the father of LSD, infamously suggested that the drug be put into the drinking water! Looking back now, in post 9/11 America, with wars in Iraq, and Afghanistan, the butchery continuing in Ukraine, Jihadist slaughter of the innocent at regular intervals the rise of Neo Nazism promoting racial hatred, economic collapse and record level illiteracy, poverty, gang warfare and massive drug problems has gradually dismantled the naive optimism that inheres this view of the human self.

In continental Europe there has been a more realistic view of human personality. Freud's idea of the barely civilised animal that is the human being, driven by destructive, selfish and utterly narcissistic concerns reined in by conscience in a psychic battle royal has always had a better pedigree. In the European configuration of the self there is more room to understand the problem of human evil, not as some accidental aberration, but rather as an intrinsic possibility of all humans. In this formulation self-actualisation can lead to the actualisation of evil.

That said, a modified understanding of self-actualisation has great value when we approach the question of meaning and purpose in life. The central notion in self-actualisation is that our life task is to express and make actual in the world our unique self. The great mistake in the early formulations by Rogers and Maslow is that self-actualisation is: firstly, a foregone conclusion if the circumstances are right, and secondly it will result in an ethical and positive human being. In fact, Maslow believes that this is a fundamental need of human beings. Almost all the evidence available suggests otherwise. It appears to me that actualising your true self in the world is an extraordinarily difficult task. It requires profound self-knowledge, great courage and a vigorous engagement with life.

Perhaps the strongest evidence available as to whether or not the world is full of people with a need or even desire to actualise themselves comes from the study of human evil. Any approach to the issue of self-development and personal growth that does not do justice to the presence of evil in the world is inadequate. Human destructiveness is far too pervasive to be left to one side in any discussion of how we approach the subject of how to live. A great deal of research into the problem of evil has occurred in the aftermath of the Holocaust. This research tells us much about how people make choices, and how susceptible we are to becoming destructive, both to our own lives and those of others. The findings about how ordinary people, you and I, can become carriers of great evil reveal an extraordinary weakness in human beings when it comes to the challenge to hold on to our moral and ethical standards. These are, in turn, crucial aspects of the true self.

In general, this research tells us that human beings, you and I, are, to a large extent conformist. Much of what is identified as research into evil is in fact a study of conformity, obedience, fearfulness, role identification and role diffusion. Stanley Milgram's experiment on conformity laid waste to much of the optimism that came from self-psychology. His experiments showed that ordinary people could be made to carry out acts of great cruelty simply because they trusted the authority figure giving the instructions. His experiments involved telling volunteers that they were partaking in a teaching project. Their job was to deliver electric shocks to the subject of the experiment who was in an adjoining room. The subject of in the experiment was in fact an actor who had to scream in pain when the shock was delivered (no actual shocks were involved but the volunteers didn't know this). The dial of the shock machine operated by the volunteers was divided into levels of lethality, up to an including possible fatal levels. All the volunteers delivered shocks, believing that the recipient was suffering, and some delivered shocks that they believed were potentially fatal. When Milgram interviewed the volunteers afterwards, most were upset, and showed that upset even when delivering the shocks. But, they still did it.

What Milgram discovered in the laboratory is borne out in real life by the story of a relief battalion of German reserve policemen sent to exterminate a village of Polish Jews during the Second World War. Christopher Browning, in an extraordinary piece of work, returned decades later to interview the policemen involved. He discovered that the battalion of reserve police comprised ordinary everyday reserve policemen in Hamburg. At that time, Hamburg was one of least anti-Semitic cities in Germany. The reserve police were just that, they held no strong ideologies; they were ordinary men earning a few extra deutschmarks in their spare time. In the main, they were family men with no axe to grind against the Jews nor anybody else for that matter.

In any modern European city, they would fit the stereotype of the traffic warden.

Within two weeks of transferring as a support unit for the German army proper these men we slaughtering defenceless Jewish men women and children. They took them from their homes, rounded them up to a central meeting point and then marched them in groups to a nearby forest. After forcing them to lie face down shot them in the back of the head. The one thing the officers failed to get these ordinary men to do was to separate the children and babies from their mothers. This, it appears, was an aspect of their empathy for others that was too hardwired into the psyche to be broken by the need to obey and conform. They allowed the children and babies to be slaughtered with their mothers!

Many vomited and cried after their deeds, but they still did them. In time some of these men began to enjoy their 'work', but they were in the minority. Browning makes the insightful conclusion that in the case of wanton brutality "brutalisation was not the cause but the effect of these men's behaviour".

Another study by psychologist Philip Zimbardo adds to our understanding of just how difficult it is to maintain one's own independent identity in the face of pressure to conform. The Stanford prison experiment was a study of the psychological effects of becoming a prisoner or prison guard. The experiment was conducted over the period of one week in August, 1971 by a team of researchers led by psychology professor Philip Zimbardo at Stanford University. It was funded by a grant from the U.S. Office of Naval Research and was of interest to both the US Navy and Marine Corps in order to determine the causes of conflict between military guards and prisoners.

In the study twenty-four students were selected out of 75 to play the prisoners and live in a mock prison in the basement of the Stanford psychology building. Roles were assigned randomly. The participants adapted to their roles well beyond what even Zimbardo himself expected, leading the "officers" to display authoritarian measures and ultimately to subject some of the prisoners to torture. In turn, many of the prisoners developed passive attitudes and accepted physical abuse, and, at the request of the guards, (played by students) readily inflicted punishment on other prisoners who attempted to stop it. The experiment even affected Zimbardo himself, who, in his capacity as "Prison Superintendent", lost sight of his role as psychologist and permitted the abuse to continue as though it were a real prison. Five of the 'prisoners' were upset enough by the process to quit the experiment early, and the entire experiment was abruptly stopped after only six days instead of the originally scheduled fourteen. That day, Zimbardo called both the "guards" and "inmates" to a meeting and announced that the 'prison' was closing down. The experimental process and the results remain controversial.

This study demonstrates the impressionability and obedience of people when provided with an ideology they accepted and social and institutional support. The guards and prisoners adapted to their roles more completely than expected, as Zimbardo himself also did, stepping beyond the boundaries of what had been predicted and leading to dangerous and psychologically damaging situations. One-third of the guards were judged to have exhibited "genuine sadistic tendencies", while many prisoners were emotionally traumatized—five of them had to be removed from the experiment early. Realizing that he had been passively allowing unethical acts to be performed under his direct supervision, Zimbardo concluded that both prisoners and guards had become too grossly absorbed in their roles and terminated the experiment after six days.

The results of these experiments are often used to support the idea that the situation caused the participants' behaviour, rather than anything inherent in their individual personalities. I disagree with this conclusion. The situation did not cause these effects, nor was there any particular destructive or evil aspects to most of the individuals; rather it reveals that, in general, people do not have very strong robust sense of their own values. Their sense of self is in fact hugely compromised by their surroundings. In a civilized world a great number of people mistakenly believe that their civilized attitudes are their own. In reality they are simply conforming to their civilised surroundings, the shared values of the populace. Take them into a cruel and destructive context and many, if not most, will succumb to the pressure to conform to a new regime of intolerance, cruelty and violence toward others. The happenings in Germany during WWII support this understanding.

All of the above tells us that human beings are very fragile in terms of their corruptibility. It tells us that most manage to get away without having to confront their weakness, lack of well-considered values, courageous commitment to their own developed ethical standards. When the Holocaust came, it revealed something, not just about the German citizenry of the 1940's, it revealed something about the fragile and weak nature of the constructed selves in the developed societies of that era, one which continues today. Renowned philosopher Hannah Arendt, echoed a similar sentiment when she wrote, "The sad truth of the matter is that most evil is done by people who never made up their minds to be or do either good or evil."

Getting to know your true self.

Self-actualisation then is rare. The examined life, and the pursuit of authenticity are challenges that can be avoided by the majority. Knowing the true self is not an accurate science. It is not a simple matter of just doing whatever comes to mind. It requires self-reflection, it requires awareness and it requires a commitment to deepen your understanding of who you are. There are some tools that can help with this exploration. Like an archaeologist you must be prepared to mark out a site for exploration and then carefully begin to dig deeper into the psyche to discover its secrets. Sometimes this is best done with the aid of someone who helps in these matters, counsellors, coaches, and spiritual guides. The following are some broad suggestions that you can use.

Uniqueness

The values of compliance, self-sacrifice and conformity were the compass that guided the parenting and training of children, as well as the rewarding and acceptance of adulthood. If you are to engage in living with authenticity you will need to address the power that these values still hold over you. Freedom to live an authentic life sometimes requires that you challenge these values by examining where they came from and why you hold them. It may mean replacing them with different ones that are based on growing awareness of your own individuality. It means accepting that you are important. It means acknowledging that your life is primarily your own. It means recognising that you can (with hard work and practice) learn how to influence and create a great deal of what goes to make up your life. Before discussing how this can be done, we must first examine what it means to be unique

Unique Genes

Being a unique human being is no mystery. Every organism that is born of sexual reproduction is unique in its genetic inheritance with the exception of identical offspring resulting in the splitting of the fertilised egg after fertilisation. This unique genetic inheritance is the beginning of personal uniqueness. Professor Steve Jones describes this uniqueness when he says of findings of genetic research: "Most important, they gave the first insight into the uniqueness of the individuals; of the existence of massive amounts of inherited diversity Their variation is such that (with the exception of identical twins) everyone alive today is unlike everyone else—and unlike everyone who has ever lived or ever will live". That genetic difference, which separates you from all others is the beginning of the quest to live a unique life.

One of the more common pervasive myths is that all people are created equally. This is an unfortunate illusion that is not borne out by reality. In modern civilised society there is an aspiration that all people should be treated equally when it comes to civil rights. That is however a long way from the notion that all people are equal. John Rawls, one of the most eminent political philosophers of the twentieth century is far more realistic about the life effects of genetic inheritance. He coined the term 'natural lottery' to describe the 'luck' that is involved in individual inborn characteristics. There is plenty of psychological research that shows how certain inherited characteristics affect a person's life. One striking example is that called the Halo effect.

The Halo effect is a common psychological phenomenon whereby if a person is seen to have a particular positive, or negative characteristic, then people tend to attribute other positive/negative qualities to that individual, in the absence of any evidence that he/she has such qualities. Thus, for example, if an individual is endowed with physical attraction (within the cultural norms of what is considered attractive), that person will be attributed a host of other positive characteristics whether they have them or not. Studies of employment interviews show that if an individual is physically attractive, they are more likely to be considered intelligent, and more likely to get the job even if physical attractiveness is not part of the job requirement. We can see this at work in the film industry where physical attractiveness is connected to moral goodness and virtue. The bad characters are almost always depicted as physically ugly

Genetic inheritance then is an important factor in unique self-hood. It is unfortunate that so little emphasis is placed of this reality within the self-help industry. Perhaps, it runs counter to the delusion being sold that anybody can become whatever they want. Genetic inheritance means that life begins with the odds for success stacked in one's favour, or not. For some then the passage through life can be far smoother. This does not however guarantee that they will make best use of their unearned advantages.

Unique Life Experience

This unique genetic inheritance is only the beginning of personal uniqueness. On top of it comes life experience and the learning that it brings. Let's take the following example:

Identical twin boys go out to play and climb a tree. One falls out of the tree and breaks his leg. He now has an experience that is different from his twin brother. In time he may become more cautious because he has experienced pain as well as the excitement that comes with curiosity, risk taking, and engagement with his environment. This timidity may greatly affect his life. On one hand he may avoid a more serious accident later on, or on the other, he may miss out on great opportunities because of his fear. His brother may, however, be paralysed for life in a later situation because he was overconfident, or then again, he may become a celebrated wildlife explorer. This example helps us to understand that our unique individuality is a combination of our inherited characteristics and our experiences in the formative periods of our lives.

Another enormous consideration in understanding how a unique life is shaped is that of the social context into which one is born. There are always exceptions to every rule. A child born in a sinkhole estate, to drug addicted/alcoholic parents who are third generation unemployed living on welfare and deprived of any means of escape for themselves, may survive and manage to climb out of the cess pit. He/she may go on to flourish in his/her life, to gain an education, to excel at some sport or creative talent. He/she may in fact become a beacon to others, a light that shines and says, the human spirit is undefeatable, and we can overcome all circumstances. I recently read such an account in the extraordinary memoir "Poor" by Katriona O' Sullivan. Another memoir in the same vein is that of Tara Westover's 'Educated'. These are inspirational stories and so worth reading. However, when we witness such triumph, it has a powerful impact primarily because it is extraordinary.

Most children born into this type of environment simply repeat in their own lives what they see around them. That is an unfortunate fact of life. And it makes the argument for the importance of ethical leadership and compassionate social planning from those in power. It is important to recognise this reality when we speak of the possibilities of living a unique and authentic life. It is naive and trite to suggest that social context does not have an enormous effect of how a human being constructs his/or her life. How then should we approach the task of understanding our unique self, that special blend of genetic temperament allied with early life experience. The following suggests three possible aids to reflecting on this issue.

Childhood Fantasy

Most often our childhood fantasies are a rich source of understanding of our true self. These fantasies are usually less clouded by the demands and restrictions of tribal cohesion. They occur before the rational self has developed to the point where practical considerations are most important. (I am not suggesting here that practicality is unimportant). Inside these fantasies there are themes that reflect your true nature. What drew your attention when you were growing up? What pictures formed in your mind? If you take time to look back at these you may find that there are common themes running through them. Some people attest that even as early as four or five they had dreams of becoming explorers, teachers, doctors and so on and so forth. We need to be cautious here though because we run the risk of continuing the myth that everybody can become extraordinary. These words are bandied around to the point of meaninglessness. "Extraordinary" means what it says: extra from the ordinary. It is absurd to say that everybody is extraordinary. Our fantasy life is often magical and impractical. We dream of the spectacular and most of us, for example, do not dream of becoming janitors when we grow up!! That said, the hints and little sparks of wisdom about ourselves can lead us to finding a direction that best suits our nature. As we follow in that direction, we find a basis for self-worth that feels very different from one that is imposed upon us by others. James Hillman in his book "The Soul's Code" gives many examples of very early childhood dreams that resembled the achievements reached in adulthood among some who reached fame in many walks of life, science, music, literature and the like. So as children, our imaginations may already be revealing a calling to us.

Peak Experiences

Another field of consciousness that you can begin to explore in self-understanding is to remember what are called peak experiences. Abraham Maslow, one of the founding fathers of self-psychology, described what he called 'peak experiences. These are described as special moments of joy, excitement and fulfilment and are marked by a sense of completion or great satisfaction. But, of course, there are peak experiences throughout our early life. There is, I believe at the centre of our psyche, a way of knowing that something is satisfying a deep need for meaning. This is not simply a "happy" feeling: it is more like a sense of achievement, completion or contentment: A feeling that you are in the right place. Even as children we can have these experiences. And, as we reflect on these, we notice again some common themes emerging. For some it will be a memory of creating something, an afternoon of focused attention and struggle to make a spaceship, a dress for a doll, a collage or a painting. On completion there is a sense that some deep part of the self has been touched. For another it will be winning the race at school sports, or being the captain of the soccer team. Then again for another it will be simply sitting in the sand dunes listening to the waves while the other children play football on the beach. There are simple experiences usually sprinkled throughout our childhood years that attest to our unique nature and carry hints for us about a life task that will fulfil us. We can also encounter these experiences as adults. When we do we should pay close attention to the situation that gives rise to this experience as it will most likely be telling us something of importance as it relates to our life task.

Others who we admire.

A third useful field to explore is to consider what it is we admire in the world. When you reflect on those you admire you discover that there are common themes, certain characteristics that these people have in common. Most of us will choose people that are in the public eye, celebrities who may be living or dead but who have a persona depicted in history or in the media. What is important here, is not how accurate the picture is. In Ireland in the 60's the picture of the pope adorned our mantelpieces alongside that of John F Kennedy. People here in Ireland did not know at that time that he was an inveterate womaniser; they were unaware of his links to some very suspect people. The image we had was inaccurate. What is important is the significance of the values we upheld in having his picture there, we valued him as a great leader, orator, family man, charming, intelligent, Catholic and so on and so forth. The people we respond to with consistent admiration and respect are often reflecting some important aspects of our own aspirations. Then again, we can admire others who are relatively unknown, who took a part in our lives for a period and left a lasting effect for the good. A teacher who inspired, a loving grandparent, a childhood friend. It is important to bring these to mind and to examine the characteristics that stimulated our admiration.

By taking time to analyse the qualities of those we admire we get a clearer picture of the values we need to actualise in our own lives to be fulfilled. We do not of course have to emulate greatness to live successfully. We do however need to access a level of freedom so as to be able to make choices that direct our lives, both in terms of what we create and in terms of the people to whom we relate

Summary

This chapter concerned itself with the challenge of understanding the difference between the constructed self and the authentic self. Like most things human it is not as simple as it sounds. There is always an overlap between the self that we create for the world and the self that lies beneath the surface. There are hidden potentialities, unexplored possibilities in every human being. Authentic living is spending our time and energy continuing to nurture the growth of all as many aspects of the true self that we can. In order to do this however, we need to have the power to make choices and decisions that open up our lives, rather than choices and decisions that trap, limit and close us down. This challenge: to enhancing our freedom and empowerment is the subject of the next chapter.

Chapter 3
Authentic Decision Making.

'Man becomes truly human only at the moment of decision.
Paul Tillich

Introduction

In this chapter I will examine the issue of freedom because it plays such a central role in changing our lives. Freedom is the absolute essential starting point and it is the aspect that must be nurtured if you are to alter any significant aspect of your life. Are you free to become the person you want to be? Do you truly have a choice or choices that will make a difference in your life, your happiness and fulfilment?

Josephine sits in front of me. It is our first meeting. After a few preliminary comments and the normal nervousness of the occasion she takes a deep breath and says "I am here because I feel completely powerless. I have lost control of my life to the point where there are times that I cannot even speak". She then describes the very real phenomenon of losing her voice, of finding herself in a situation where she cannot speak. She is traumatized by a relationship she is in but can find no way out. As each year passes her ability to cope is further weakened, leaving her less able to consider getting away from her abusive partner. Her worries for her children are a major part of what is holding her, and yet I sense that even without them she would find it extremely difficult to get free of this relationship.

As we continue in our dialogue, she strikes me as a very capable person. She is articulate, well read, expressive and intelligent. Once again, I am reminded of how easily any of us, no matter how capable, can come to a point in our life where we feel that we have no control. In other words, we lose our freedom, or more accurately, we give it away. Over a period of weeks, we gradually navigate the history of the relationship. Unsurprisingly, Josephine cancels a session and then stops showing up. Our task to rebuild her sense of personal power is sabotaged for now. The challenge to rediscover her freedom was too costly for her at this time.

Another lady attending a personal development seminar gets angry with me. The seminar is held in a community centre in a small village in the West of Ireland, surrounded by a fairly bleak landscape, noted for high poverty levels, and massive emigration. She is angry that I speak of making choices. She tells me it's not that simple. And of course, she is right. I see in her demeanour a lifetime of struggle and toil. I hear in her voice a despair that reflects her belief that she is trapped and can find no way to escape the contingencies and conditions of her life. Attending the personal development seminar was, for her, a bit like going to the cinema, a pleasant distraction to fill a winter's evening. It was not supposed to challenge her and discomfort her in this way. She does not believe that she has lost her freedom; she feels she never had any.

Losing freedom, on one hand, or never developing it, on the other, are conditions of the human spirit that contribute enormously to personal suffering. Without freedom we are lost. We are simply living out our lives chained in some kind of slavery. As Rousseau, that most romantic of philosophers says "man is born free but everywhere is in chains". These chains may take many forms. Some of the more prevalent ones are connected to fear, such as fear of self-expression, fear of rejection, or fear of being abandoned. These fears drive a person into choosing safety above all else. Our freedom can also be crippled when we live out our lives in response to the expectations of others. The needs and expectations of our spouse, partner, family, neighbours, colleagues or friends can completely dominate our lives. As we have seen in the previous chapter there are many kinds of social pressures that cause us to betray our own needs, hopes, beliefs and desires to the point where we are simply a construction made in the image and likeness of others. Other chains are less personal such as the chains of poverty, and social deprivation. Those who are disenfranchised, for whatever reason, from access to the requirements of living some kind of quality of life can find themselves lost and despairing.

When we are living in ways that undermine our freedom, we always know that there is something wrong. This knowing also takes many forms. For some it is a gut feeling, for others, a vague unease and for still others a chronic sadness and despair. For some it is a constant bitterness evoked by the belief that they have been dealt a bad hand at the table of life whilst everyone else seems to hold some trumps. All of these experiences can be reduced to the experience of loss of freedom to live as we desire. It is to this issue that Thoreau's famous comment is best suited, "the mass of men live lives of quiet desperation".

Becoming Free.

What is freedom? In essence, freedom is that faculty that allows us to change things. Such changes may be to the external world, such as our environment, our work, our relationships etc, or may be more internal, our attitudes, perspectives and feelings. Change then is the key outcome of the practice of freedom. Before developing further on this theme I wish to discuss a "theory" abounding in the Self-Help/ Body-Mind-Spirit world that presents a view of freedom that is both delusional and dangerous.

One of the great illusions of modern self-help movement is that we are utterly free. This is reflected in the ideas that everything that happens to us is in some way a consequence of our thinking or behaviour. This view can be best summarised by the prevalent phrase "you are the creator of your own reality". This idea is reflected in some way shape or form in almost all recent writings in the areas of personal development. Some of the vaguer renditions suggest that you create your reality by way of positive or negative transfer of energy through your mental attitude. Examples abound of people being told that whatever you send out to the universe is returned to you. It works like this. If you are afraid of something: rejection, bankruptcy, failure, or disease for example, and you spend time ruminating about such an event then you are in some way feeding it with negative energy. This strengthens it and makes it more likely to become a reality. In this way you have created the reality you didn't want. In summary, if you worry a lot, then bad things will come true (very cold comfort for a worrier). And it will be your own doing.

Others are blunter when they tell you that when you choose a behaviour you also choose the consequences. This approach is more pragmatic. It suggests that most of what happens to you is your own responsibility. Personally, I think that is daft. Our intentions are a large part of our choices. If I choose to hurry across the road, the consequence I am intending is to get to the other side quickly, often so that I can reach my goal and, for example, post that letter before the deadline for collection. The fact that I trip on the road because I am hurrying and am hit by a truck that leaves me paralyzed for life had no relation whatever to my choice to hurry.

The theory of freedom, namely how we make things happen, in the New Age thinking is a combination of three beliefs, those about the power of thought, a quasi-religious doctrine called the Universal Law of Attraction, and the notion that humans being are able to "Manifest their Reality" The following is a description and critique of these concepts so that they can be cleared away as offering any useful or productive understanding of freedom. I am setting out this critique because the ideology built into this self-help movement is damaging people's lives, and more specifically undermining how to exercise and expand personal freedom. Sometimes it is as important to identify the wrong paths as it is to indicate the right ones.

The Power of Thought

The last few decades have seen a growing interest in the power of thought to affect one's quality of life. In most of the self-help literature there is at least some reference that your thinking is a crucial part of your well-being. In general, this is true. There is, however, a more recent twist in how thinking is defined and understood. The power of thought no longer simply means that your thinking affects your outlook, focus, and mood. The power of thought is now believed to have some kind of magical influence on the external world. This new and rather fantastic claim offers great hope to people. It is also in my opinion a delusion. Let us take a closer look.

It has been shown that the way people think about things can have powerful effects on the way they approach life and the way that they feel from one day to the next. The whole basis for cognitive/behaviour therapy is grounded in the understanding that changing the way we think will affect our quality of life. Anyone interested in a much more substantive and well thought out approach to the way that thinking influences our lives should look at the work of the pioneers in this area: Albert Ellis and Aaron Beck.

One of the best examples of the power of thought is found in what is called the placebo effect. This has been formally recognised around the medical and scientific communities for more than fifty years. It is clear that when a person is given to believe that a medicine is treating some ailment, even if the medicine is simply a sugar pill, a significant number of patients will report an alleviation of symptoms. Some important insights into how this works are worth mentioning. The first being that the illness or symptoms that are most susceptible to the placebo effect are those that are, in fact, psychosomatic: in other words, there may be no organic problem to begin with. Changing the belief alleviates the symptoms thereby curing the illness that had in fact no organic basis.

Additionally, many depressed people who are given a placebo instead of an active medication will get better. There are many reports of physical healing and remissions taking place by way of treatment with a placebo. How is this possible? How can belief that one is being treated for an illness actually have a physical effect? The obvious answer lies in the function of the immune system, which is the body's armoury against disease.

It is well documented that stress depletes the immune systems and thus weakens our battle against disease as well as compromising the effectiveness of recovery when we are laid low. Hope and positive action are good for combating stress. Anything that improves our levels of hope, confidence and positive mindset thus relieves stress which, in turn, prevents the damage to our immune system and also maximises our healing powers. Thinking therefore has a physical impact by indirectly improving our powers of recovery. It should be said, however, that the great impact of the power of thought is in reversing the effects of other thoughts. In other words, conditions that are directly produced by the mind, are impacted more effectively by the mind. All of this confirms what is known within psychology and medicine about the power of thought for decades, and, in a less scientific context, since we left the caves. The power of suggestion is as old as Methuselah.

So far so good. Now we move to the next stage of expanding this reasonable and well-researched fact into the area of fantasy and illusion. This stage is based on the conceptualisation of thought as a form of energy. The nature of thought is a profoundly complex puzzle which is beyond the scope of this book to fully explore. Our brains work by electricity. MRI (magnetic resonance imaging) scans work on this very principle. Thinking is dependent on the transmission of electrical pulses among brain cells

After the disclosure of the kind of research findings described above, as well as the progress of quantum physics, some elements of the self-help world took off into a world of delusion with regard to the power of thought. It is important to slay the illusions that emerged in consequence, otherwise you could spend years living in false hope that your thoughts will bring about magical changes in your life and life circumstances.

One of the most popular publications that perhaps best exemplify the delusions about the power of thought is that of "The Secret" by Australian Journalist Rhonda Byrne. Some examples from this book are useful in portraying what is now a generally held view expressed throughout a lot of the self-help/body-Mind-Spirit literature, which is having a very definite effect on those who embrace its philosophy. The examples here concern two areas that often emerge as cultural values of acceptability and self-worth. These are: (i) physical beauty, and (ii) material wealth. I am reminded of a comment made by a friend when I told him I was considering writing this book. He commented to make sure that if I wanted a commercial success in the self-help industry I should remember the two words "RICH and THIN". Anything that tells people how to get rich or to lose weight, even if it doesn't work will sell. "The Secret" tells us precisely how this can be done. And it has sold several million copies as well as producing a whole industry of spin-off products. I would not begrudge its success if it really did work, if, as the Ronseal advertisement say, "It does exactly what it says on the tin". Unfortunately for those sucked into its irrational and misleading promises, it doesn't.

How to lose weight? In a world where the beauty industry constantly shames women who are carrying more weight than is healthy for them, this book offers the following jewel of wisdom. "The most common thought that people hold, and I held it too, is that food was responsible for my weight gain. That is a belief that does not serve you, and in my mind now is complete balderdash. <u>Food is not responsible for putting on weight</u>. It is your thought that food is responsible for putting on weight that actually has food put on weight. Remember, thoughts are primary cause of everything, and the rest is effects from those thoughts. Think perfect thoughts and the result must be perfect weight. Let go all those limiting thoughts. Food cannot cause you to put on weight unless you think it can." (underline mine) (p.59).

It is difficult to believe that otherwise intelligent people, with a normal quota of common sense could be led into such delusion? (Apparently yes, and in great numbers). Anyone who has ever worked with or known people who have problems with weight through overeating can see immediately the folly of this kind of thinking. It is, of course, great news for those afflicted with eating disorders, that food won't make you fat. No need to run to the bathroom after meals! Just think thin. In a society where obesity is rampant, it is at the very least, irresponsible to send out this message. It is also an extraordinary insult to rational thinking to deny that the obesity crisis that is bedevilling the world is not related to the food industry. All of the studies show that cheap, highly processed food is a central part of the obesity crisis, and poverty is a part of that phenomenon. Poor people buy cheap food.

If you do not have an organic illness such as diabetes or some hormonal imbalance and you are significantly overweight then it is most likely that you are eating too much of the wrong food, drinking too much alcohol, and not getting enough exercise. That's it. That's the simple part. The difficult part is that eating/drinking habits are strongly connected to personal life circumstances, financial resources, emotional make-up and so on and so forth. And these are often very difficult to change.

Certainly, your attitude of mind and the way you think about yourself will have considerable impact on your eating habits. This is not, however, what we are being told. We are being sold the fiction that your thoughts themselves have a direct impact on the way your body metabolises food for energy. In other words if you are five stone overweight, if you regularly suck down a litre of soda, snuffle up daily fries, chips, burgers, top it off with some ice cream, and have a little snack of peanut butter and jelly at night, as long as you focus your thoughts that the food will not make you fat, then you will not gain weight!

How to get rich? Elsewhere in this book, and others like it, we see something similar in relation to money and wealth. We live in a world full of people who have damaged their lives by overspending, by getting loans that they cannot repay and who have succumbed to the extraordinarily strong temptations promoted by credit card companies only to find themselves trapped in debt with little hope of extricating themselves. To these unfortunates, good news is on the way. Here it is, gratis of similar encouragement by "wealth coach" David Schimer. He tells us that his success with "The Secret" began when he 'thought' his way out of financial trouble. The technique involved taking each bill that arrived in the mail and telling himself it was a cheque. Soon the cheques began to roll in and he is now a very wealthy man. We are not told where the cheques came from. Thinking that bills are cheques is in the same family of delusion as thinking that too much food won't make you fat. In the world I inhabit this kind of thinking is akin to a psychiatric disorder.

What about disease and illness? No problem. Here's the solution. "Our physiology creates disease to give us feedback, to let us know that we have an imbalanced perspective, or we are not being loving or grateful". And "when a person has manifested a disease in the body temple or some kind of discomfort in their life, can it be turned around through the power of right thinking? Absolutely yes" (p.128). A couple of points here are useful. First, you will notice that disease is supposed to be telling us something, and also that you are manifesting it in some way or other. This means in essence that you are responsible for causing your illness. This theme abounds in the modern pseudo-spiritual world of today's self-help market. When I read these authors, I am left to wonder if they have any understanding or true compassion for the reality of human suffering, for the complex nature of life in the cycle of living and dying. I wonder do they have any sense at all of what human biology is about; any concept of bacteriology or the immune system? It is incredible that such delusions are not only promoted, but are accepted by millions of people.

Does your thinking make you ill? Sometimes. It is well known (by virtue of orthodox science) that stress suppresses the immune system. A suppressed immune system has more difficulty in fighting disease. Therefore, stressful living can lead to illness. And it is also known that living a stressful life is sometimes the result of bad choices and ignorance. It is however absurd to consider that disease is a function of negative thinking, and that healing is about reversing those thoughts. Let us take the AIDS virus or the COVID 19 pandemic for example. How does "The Secret" apply to diseases that killed tens of millions of people.? Try this gem from Rhonda Byrne "You cannot 'catch' anything unless you think you can, and thinking you can is inviting it to you with your thought" (p.132). As for the cure for those who attracted AIDS by negative thinking (as distinct from sharing needles or having unprotected sex, or simply catching the Covid virus in the local supermarket), here is a gift from "The Secret". "You don't have to fight to get rid of a disease. Just the simple process of letting go of negative thoughts will allow your natural state of health to emerge within you. And your body will heal itself" (p.134).

It is grossly irresponsible to tell people that nothing is incurable. The very science that has led to the great breakthroughs in modern medicine and pain management would swiftly dismiss the outrageous claims made about health, illness, and treatment in books such as this. Professor Jonathan Singer tells us that "the great successes of modern medicine have created for many the mirage that human longevity can be increased indefinitely, that maybe there is even a gene that can be manipulated to turn off death...The science of biology, however serves as a check on these irrationalities".

Do you know what you are going to die from yet? Unlikely. I don't myself know what is going to kill me. I could hazard some guess given my family history of colon cancer. Then again it could be something catastrophic like a car accident. Let me recount an incident that recently came to my attention. On this New Year's evening a group of people met together at their local church in a small town in the United States. They gathered together for prayer and worship and to give thanks for the year gone by and to celebrate the beginning of the coming one. A mother brought her little four-year-old son to the Christian celebration. He had a winning cherubic smile shining out of his big brown eyes. A mile away from the church another party was in session. A more raucous affair which involved celebratory firing off of guns, most likely legally held. One individual fired his/her AK 47 into the air. The bullet soared high into the firmament, gradually lost momentum, turned on its arc of descent, gathered speed from gravity, found its way through the roof of the church and into the little boy's head killing him.

With all out brilliant technology, we do not have any system that could track the line of a bullet like that. But it is these events that happen every day, where death and destruction are part of our human condition. The quasi philosophy of 'the Secret' and its ilk gives us nothing by way of dealing with tragedy except to suggest that somehow, we are responsible for it. The notion that the contingencies of everyday life is a simple product of our thinking is almost laughable. That is, if so many people did not embrace it as a way of life or at least as a way of making sense of life.

One of the most erudite descriptions of the cultural phenomenon is given by Barbara Ehrenreich in her book." Smile or Die; How Positive Thinking Fooled America and The World". There she described how her own cancer diagnosis led her to experience how this ideology is applied to cancer patients and, in her experience, how it can be so pernicious, leaving vulnerable people stranded and alienated if they do not embrace the ideology. Through that experience she then researched how the ideology has penetrated almost all walks of life from business, psychotherapy and religion.

Modern medicine successfully treats many illnesses that originally killed people. As a result of these successes life in general is prolonged, at least in the developed world. This means that we are going to sample more diseases which will be successfully treated before we eventually die. Let's get real here. Dying is inevitable and most times it is through the eventual wearing out of the body which eventually allows some disease or other take us out. Modern medicine did not cure my father's cancer, but it did allow him to avoid dying in agony, something that would not have been available to him a century ago.

I have taken the above examples to highlight the vulnerability of people to believe 'the power of magical thinking' The power of thought as presented in many recent 'New Age' publications are encouraging people to embrace the notion of magical thinking. Widespread acceptance of this idea will lead to a great dumbing down of the challenge involved in real life change. It leads to a failure to act responsible for your life. It will result in wasted years and a great deal of disillusionment. Your thoughts are important and are powerful in a very limited way. They provide very important guidance for how to live your life. For the most part they do not, in themselves, change anything.

Thinking is, however, the most important faculty in pursuing the task of the examined life. It is the faculty that allows you to approach and understand the following questions. These are the central questions that confront any person who wishes to live an authentic life. The first is the question, who are you? From this comes the other central challenges that concern how to express your unique self in the world, what to create that gives you a sense of purpose and meaning, what experiences provide fulfilment and satisfaction, what kind of people to invite to the table of your life. These questions are at the heart of authentic living. They are big questions and are not helped in any way by a trite and superficial theory of the power of thought discussed above. I realise I am labouring this point somewhat, but I do so because, tempting as it is to embrace this ideology, it will not further your path to authenticity if you get captured by it.

Freedom within Limitations

If then we cannot take recourse to blind faith in a magical universe that will make our wishes come true, where does that leave us? For centuries, philosophers, intellectuals and theologians have argued about the nature of freedom. Many argued that there's no such thing. In their view we are intelligent creatures whose intelligence makes us arrogant enough to believe we are free when the truth is, we are simply reactors to the programming in our genetic makeup, social conditioning and environment cues. This view of human beings predominated certain aspects of psychology and psychiatry into the 1980's. It has since lost its popularity, probably because of the bleak and hopeless picture it gave us of ourselves.

It did however tell us a great truth. There are enormous limitations built into the fabric of being human. We are limited by genetics (my basketball career was over by the time I was born!!). We are limited by intellect. It is, of course, no longer politically correct to say such things. And yet it is flying in the face of reality (even consensual reality) to deny the fact that each of us has a modicum of intellectual power and some are more gifted that others. We are limited by physical strength, a limitation that only recently has less dramatic consequences for us with our more modern dependence on cognitive power and technology. We are limited by language. Whole schools of philosophy show us that our ways of thinking and experiencing reality are bounded by language. We are limited by time. I don't believe that any form of positive thinking is going to help me live forever. We are limited by culture, even as cultural influences in our formation are being eroded by the world becoming a global village. We are limited by social conditions. The popular media consistently remind us of the bias and prejudice that prevents access to economic resources, and even basic survival needs based on where you grew up, the colour of your skin and your gender.

Thus, our starting point in relation to freedom is that it is always a freedom within limitation. Any view that discounts this reality is just that popular seductive illusion based on denial and wishful thinking. You are limited in many ways. This book will not help you to deny this. It will not help you to awaken any giants (unless there is an actual one inside you, perhaps one in every few thousand readers has some untapped exceptional talent: if so congratulations!). It will not help you to live forever, or for most readers to get rich. What it may do is help you to work within the limitations of your life to expand and practice greater freedom and to continue to do so for the rest of your life. In doing so you will gradually push back the boundary lines of limitations. In time, some will no longer exist, only because they were illusory to begin with. Others will lose some of their hold on you because you can learn to surmount them. And for still others you will develop an acceptance that will help you to be at peace with them. All of this will help you to become someone who at the end of your life will face the task of dying with a sense of completion that you lived authentically. And, in the meantime you can feel more positive and enthusiastic about your life.

Choosing the road to freedom.

The experience of freedom is an absolute essential part of transforming and building your life. Do you want to become a person whose life is only marginally limited and who enjoys the enormous sense of fulfilment that comes with knowing that you are truly living your own life? If so then the first step is in learning what it means to be free.

Freedom is that human capacity to create, construct and influence the constitution of one's identity and the direction of one's life. Because it is a human capability it is prone to remain undeveloped in some and highly developed in others. Freedom is not a constant. It is not, for example, akin to the colour of our eyes or our adult height. These are characteristics that remain somewhat constant throughout our lives.

Freedom is not like that. It is more akin to physical fitness. People who are physically fit take regular exercise that strengthens the muscles, speeds up metabolism, helps ward off the deterioration of aging. In addition, they add vitamins to their diet and eat good quality food. All of these measures improve the individual's physical health and fitness. Others eat junk food, lots of fat, never exercise, drink too much alcohol and smoke cigarettes. The result is a bad physical condition. Like our physical health the condition of our sense of freedom depends on how we treat it.

Christian apologist C.S. Lewis presents a view of freedom that is helpful. *"I would much rather say that every time you make a choice you are turning the central part of you, the part that chooses into something a little different from what it was before. And taking your life as a whole, with all your innumerable choices, all your life long you are slowly turning this central thing either into a heavenly creature or into a hellish one...One kind of creature is heaven, that is it is joy and peace and knowledge and power. To be the other means madness, horror, idiocy, rage, impotence and eternal loneliness. Each of us at each moment is progressing to the one state or the other"*.

This description is stern and moralistic but it captures for me the essence of freedom, a gradual life long process of creating your individual personhood through innumerable choices. Our choices can lead us to become healthy, open-minded, sincere, gentle, successful and much more. It can also lead us to become judgemental, greedy, hurtful dangerous and trapped. Once we accept that we have the capacity for choice we are faced immediately with the responsibility to use it and to accept that we are to some extent responsible for the person we have become. If we have made successive choices that lead us to dim the light of our lives then we have to take responsibility for that outcome.

I spoke recently with a young man of 20: A gentle and sensitive soul who experiences life as difficult and painful. As we talked, he described his experience of his father leaving his family when he was just eight years old. In the absence of his father this young man began to take responsibility for his younger sisters and despite a close bond with his father saw his relationship with him wither and die. His father abandoned him for a new wife and her children. They became his new family and he no longer took an interest in his own children. This loss of his father had a devastating effect on this young man's life.

From the father's viewpoint he may have had some good reason for letting go of his relationship with his children. Maybe his anger with his wife, his need to please his new partner or his busy life all created the circumstances that led to his choice to ignore the needs of his son. No matter what set of circumstances were involved, he made consistent, often very simple choices that eventually added up to his failure as a father. He had to choose to not make the odd phone call to reassure this young man that he was important to him. Not choosing is a choice. When birthdays came around, he had to choose not to celebrate the day, at weekends he had to choose to not arrange to watch the football together, or go fishing for an hour or so. None of these are big decisions, but put together they have an enormous outcome. A young man whose life is deeply scarred, and a father who has missed out on one of life's greatest blessings, a loving relationship with his child.

My own father had a lovely phrase that captures how significant the little choices can be for both good and ill. He'd often say after some calamity in the workshop, "Michael, it's a small thing that can spoil a man's shirt". The small things can add up to a great effect. Once you know this then you can realise that gradual decisions can add up to a changed life. That is what it means to be free.

Another aspect that is worth describing is that the very capacity to choose can be used to take away your capacity to choose. In this story Joseph is now twenty, his childhood is gone, so his father's choices led to a consequence whereby he can no longer recover his relationship with his child. The opportunity is gone. Additionally, and perhaps more importantly, his consistent neglect of his son may have resulted in his becoming a less caring father than he was at the beginning. His character may have been affected by his failure to cultivate that part of him that can reach out in love and support. Thus, his choices undermined his freedom in two ways: lost opportunity and character change.

C.S. Lewis also describes this process *"When a man is getting better, he understands more and more clearly the badness that is still left within him. When a man is getting worse, he understands his own badness less and less. A moderately bad man knows he is not very good. A thoroughly bad man thinks he is all right. This is common sense really. You understand sleep when you are awake, not when you are sleeping. You can see mistakes in arithmetic when your mind is working properly, while you are making them you cannot see them. You can understand the nature of drunkenness when you are sober not when you are drunk"* (p.83).

Our choices, then, can lead us into self-delusion. The function of self-delusion is to protect us from the discomfort of accepting when we have failed. In Joseph's story his dad was a good father to him for the early years of his life. When he left his marriage, he was a reasonably good father. Gradually as he got worse and failed his son more, he began to believe that he was doing ok or even that he was a moderately good father. As he made more and more choices that involved neglect, he changed his perception of reality to accommodate his own failure. This, in fact, seems to be the case because, in a recent conversation with his father, Joseph confronted him with his feelings of betrayal and neglect. His father became quite shocked. He offered to pay for the best counselling available, but yet did nothing to address the issue.

This type of delusional thinking is quite common. I recently heard a story of a man who embraced a meditative lifestyle after many years of searching. Part of the spiritual practice involved a belief in absent healing and other forms of prayerful meditation. Having had little contact with his children over many years he undertook to do "absent parenting" (by way of meditating using the same techniques as those in absent healing), rather than move to a closer location so that he could actually spend time with them. In his view he has been a good father to them. He chose to believe that what he was doing was in some way adequate to the needs of his children. Had he simply admitted to himself that he hadn't the will or strength to do it differently, then maybe he could have had some opportunity for real change to emerge. His self-delusion however left him with no strong sense that he was not being a good parent, and as the old saying goes, if it's not broken, don't fix it. Self-delusion leads us to believe that things are not broken when they are.

These examples highlight certain aspects of the nature of freedom. The way we exercise our freedom can diminish our freedom through lost opportunities through changes in our personality and through damaged perception of reality. In general, these occur very gradually and involve consistent and often apparently insignificant decisions, that lead to the major influences regarding the condition of one's life and character. The good news is that small changes can lead in time to a dramatically different and better life. The trick is to know what decisions to make and which choices to avoid. This is the subject of a later chapter.

We do not always choose the consequences that result from our choices, but we do choose whether or not to learn from them. And real learning always leads to some kind of change, either in our behaviour or in our attitude or both. Failing to learn from consequences is a powerful cause of suffering, failure and broken lives. When we look at our lives then we can often see a pattern of choices that we have made and ignored the consequences of gradually leading us into deeper and deeper trouble. It is in this sense that we can say that we are playing a significant role in creating the life that we now have.

The Progressive Nature of Freedom

Since you reached the age of reason you have been making choices. You have exercised your freedom and to a greater or lesser extent, you created the life you now have. No matter how many influences were at work in your decision making, whether you had faulty beliefs, wrong thinking, fear, anger, blind ambition, and/or any version of influences, that central part of you is still responsible for the decisions you have made. It is absolutely crucial to accept this. In accepting this you do not have to berate yourself if the life you now have is one of difficulty, boredom, disillusionment. You do have to acknowledge that you have played a part in creating it. When you accept this you also accept the possibility for change. The positive fact is that if you have, to some extent, created this life, then by definition, you can also change it. That is the great hope in accepting both personal freedom, and personal responsibility. If on the other hand you believe that you have had no part in the life you now live then it is unlikely that you can change it. That is the road to stagnation and despair.

Personal responsibility for your choices is the central tenet of empowering your own life. To expand your sense of freedom in order to more effectively create the life you want requires work. It is part of the naiveté of our world that suggests that personal empowerment can be bought at a weekend seminar, or by reading a book. Just as losing freedom and surrendering a life may have taken years of small defeats and little incidental betrayals, so too does it require day by day commitment and practice to become a person who is largely choosing the life they want. As in athletics, to achieve significant success a person must reach a high level of physical fitness, and in order to make significant improvements in our lives at all levels we need to have developed a high degree of freedom. To do so means we must identify what we need to do to get it working for us.

Don't despair simply because the stuff you've read and practiced doesn't work. To become a person who experiences a large degree of freedom in your life is a task that requires solid commitment. It is a great undertaking. And, like all great undertakings, it will take time, energy, courage, learning, endurance and more. Freedom is a prize. It is the Olympic gold medal of life. Nobody gets an Olympic gold medal without absolute commitment.

Commitment alone however does not get you to your destination, you also have to know the direction. One rather popular saying that is often mistakenlyattributed to Einstein goes something like "to keep on doing the same thing and expect a different outcome is a form of insanity". Most of us know people who have very high levels of commitment and are making a complete mess of their lives because they are committed to doing something that are not taking them where they need to go. Steven Covey nicely captures this concept in the question "is the ladder you are climbing leaning against the wrong wall"? He also uses the analogy of road building. Imagine that you wish to build a path through a forest. You may bring a high level of commitment and expertise to the task, but if you have chosen the wrong forest it will not matter how good the road is. Commitment alone is necessary but not sufficient. Freedom and power to change is necessary but not sufficient. It must be allied with a proper sense of direction. This issue will be dealt with in the next chapter. Here we need to examine some of the obstacles in the way of freedom.

Identifying where you are stuck

Many people have a rather simplistic approach to the things that cause them deep frustrations. Some of us simply blame someone else. If you are stuck in a dead-end job, you may blame your parents for not helping you enough with self-confidence or the more practical problem of supporting your education. If you are stuck in a lifeless marriage or relationship you might blame your partner, or yourself. If all your high ideals have crashed and burned onto the cliffs of life experience you may now feel disillusioned and cynical.

Most of us try to reach some kind of accommodation with these experiences. Maybe you are stoically and patiently trying for some acceptance. Maybe you are engaging in some spiritual practice to help you with your feelings of disillusion and despair. Maybe you are drinking too much to take the edge of your pain. Maybe you are living with a fantasy of a better life that helps distract you from the one that you inhabit day in and day out. Maybe you are reading "The Secret" or some similar quasi inspirational fare and hoping it will work. If you are doing any version of these, take a bow. You are normal.

Within this normal everyday stoicism lies a great trap. When you give up and become cynical, bitter or just plain depressed you have left the only road that can take you to where you need to go in order to be fulfilled. You have abdicated responsibility for your life because you have been defeated. You now exist rather than live. You will gradually become one whose life reflects the old phrase of "keeping on keeping on". Your life becomes a tired, complaint filled, existence.

When you replace the actual experience of your life with a fantasy version that exists only in your head you have cultivated denial to a high art. Denial is one of the more life damaging patterns because it prevents us from ever truly addressing the problems that need to be solved for us to flourish. You live a kind of Walter Mitty existence, imagining yourself as someone you are not as the years ebb away. You might wake up some day out of the half-light of your dream world and find that it's nearly all over.

When you settle for the bitter taste of blame, you can comfort yourself with the feeling that your diminished life is someone else's fault. You take yourself off the hook. The short-term gain of a comfort zone (or as a client of mine termed it "a discomfort zone") is far outweighed by the loss of any kind of fulfilled life, as well as the constellation of problems, physical and mental that go with becoming a living vessel of bitterness. The sour flavour of life turns your demeanour into a tight and twisted visage. Your immune system gets under pressure, and the tightness in your musculature bends you out of shape, often leading to chronic illness and unhappiness.

Carolyn Myss is eloquent in describing this condition "Although the state of mind is sad, self-defeating and defeatist, some people derive great power in maintaining it because it gives them permission to lead a life of minimum expectation and limited responsibility. It allows them to lean on others for assistance and to play on their guilt to keep that assistance coming. They speak regretfully or bitterly about creative goals that they cannot accomplish, now or ever, because of their history of emotional or physical abuse. They seek out a support system that gives them a social comfort zone, one that will remain sympathetic to their woundedness without ever challenging them to put it behind them. Since nothing is expected of the wounded personality, they can never fail" (p.32).

These are all different forms of being stuck. The difficulties of life, the pain of loss, the constant adversity of struggle, the crippling grip of fear, the mistaken life choices often made in ignorance can all add up to what feels like an intolerable burden from which escape is impossible and trying to be different is futile. So, if you're stuck you may have also given up. Giving up is understandable. Giving up is forgivable. Giving up is fatal. Giving up means retreating into some well-worn familiar routine that will see out your remaining years or decades in some numb and diminished life.

An important step in reclaiming freedom is making a choice that no matter how stuck you feel right now you must accept that there is a possibility for improvement. You must take a step of faith that, with the right help and guidance, with the commitment of your energy to learn and practice new ways of dealing with your life, you will find a better way to live. If you cannot promise yourself to set out on a new path starting right now, then you are not ready. Pick up a different book, preferably one that is entertaining and enjoyable. You might need more time to experience the growing voice that's telling you that it's not good enough to live like this. That little insistent call from your true self that says you were born for better than this.

Or then again maybe you are just too worn out and tired now. Perhaps you need more time. Compassion towards yourself is important. There is a case to be made for taking rest, for seeking the true meaning of asylum, a place of sanctuary to give time for healing and recovery. Just remember two things. Firstly, time is the one resource that you cannot replace. If you need more time before addressing the issue of changing your life, give yourself a deadline. Don't just drift on and on and expect some miracle cure for that which ails you. Most of us have to make our own miracles.

Secondly, most forms of giving up are seductively comfortable. I remember watching a cookery program that nicely illustrated this latter point. The celebrity chef was discussing cooking lobster and described a way to do so compassionately. This compassionate approach did not involve the usual method of dropping a live lobster into boiling water. Rather, this approach suggests that lobster be placed in a saucepan of cold water that was then put on heat. The water would gradually heat up and cause the lobster to fall asleep. Thus, the lobster would be asleep by the time the water boiled. Giving up can be a bit like this. You become more deeply unconscious (unaware) by the time you die.

To borrow from Dylan Thomas, "do not go gently into that good night but rage rage against the dying of the light". Do not go gently into a numbing diminished life. Fight for a life that is truly yours. Open yourself to learn what you need, to find out what to let go and what to take on, but first, make a commitment to yourself. This is a crucial step and every journey starts with a single step. Make a commitment to the practice of freedom. Take some time now as you read this to reflect. Make a promise to yourself that you are going to set out on a voyage of discovery. You are going to discover who you want to become. You are going to learn what you need to leave behind. You are going to pursue your dreams, after you understand what they mean. You have no idea yet how long it will take. You do not know yet the price you will be asked to pay. You do know, and you know it deep in your heart, if you do not live a life that is true to yourself you will have lost the most important challenge of all. You will have in the words of the holy writ, 'taken your hand from the plough'. You will have betrayed your life.

Freedom From and Freedom To

The coin of freedom has two sides. 'freedom from' and 'freedom to': -Freedom from- means getting free from life circumstances that are damaging your life. These circumstances are often the result of choices made at a time of immaturity or ignorance. They may exist because you made decisions out of fear, ignorance, dependency, peer pressure or some mix of all the above. 'Freedom from' means being able to move beyond these circumstances. It means being able to make new decisions, and make new choices. These new decisions and choices may have the effect of releasing you from conditions in your life in which you now feel trapped and frustrated.

Leaving behind and letting go are both essential parts of this process. They are often fraught with difficulty, and sometimes shadowed with grief. You have made a commitment to becoming free to create a life of your choosing. This means that you must now reflect on what has brought you to this point and what aspects of your life are no longer what you want. I remember, in this regard, a story told by Bernie Siegal. A successful executive in his early forties watches with growing anger his young son's resistance to eating his vegetables. At table one evening he eventually explodes with rage and shouts at his son as to why he will not eat what he is given. His son rather sheepishly replies, "because I don't want to". At this point his father explodes again and shouts "what has wanting got to do with anything? I've never done anything I want in my whole life".

The beauty of this story is that the man in question had the good sense to reflect on what he had said. He realized almost immediately the insanity that underpinned his life and that this was his problem and not his sons. Not only had he completely betrayed his own life, he was in the process of teaching his son to emulate him. This is not to deny that there are times when doing what you don't 'feel' like doing is the better way. Sometimes you really should eat your vegetables!

This man's condition, whereby he had never taken the time to understand what he truly wanted from his life, is not unusual. For many of us there is a deep and abiding prohibition lying within, sown into the fabric of the self that says that to want something for your own enjoyment and fulfilment and to pursue it, is selfish. Not only is it selfish, it is also wrong. It is the road to perdition. When it is applied to the larger issue of having a life that you want, the stakes go up even further. The inner voice of conscience says, "of course you cannot live for yourself". Your life is not yours. Your life is to be lived in the service of others. Your life belongs to God, to the community, to the Party, to the wider society and so on and so forth depending on what cultural milieu into which you have been born. Those of us who are reared within the cultural setting of strong religious ideology may have very grave difficulty with this issue. Guilt and self-deprecation soon follow any effort to begin to create a life of your own choosing and unless we address this issue the subconscious demon of guilt will sabotage all your self- development work.

Philosopher Friedrich Nietzsche brilliantly exposes many aspects of the diminishing morality that inheres much of religious based morality. His work, in particular, challenges what he sees as the morality of the slave. He notes that such morality usually comprises a series of negative commands: Thou Shalt Nots. He tells us that rarely do we find the positive commands that encourage us to flourish. My own suggestions for such a list would include: Thou Shalt make a good life for yourself. Thou Shalt seek to be loved and respected, Thou Shalt leave bad situations and people who damage you. Thou shalt cultivate abiding and affirming friendships. Thou shalt use your talents creatively. Thou shalt cultivate and pursue joy in your life., Thou shalt treat others with the kindness and respect you have for yourself. Thou shalt take responsibility for your life. These are a few that come to mind. The reader might at this point take time to write their own list.

Cultivating Personal Freedom.

Firstly, we must accept the challenge of personal freedom and personal responsibility. These two are inextricably linked. If you are free to choose what goes on in your life then you are also responsible, in part, for what you have become. Personal empowerment means learning to consider seriously the choices you make. It is essential to recognise that it is not the big choices that often change our lives, it is often the little ones that gradually add up to what appears to be a big life-changing decision. We can be left with the illusion that it was the big decision that sent us off course. Generally, it doesn't work like that. Let us look at some examples that could clarify this issue.

The film, "Any Given Sunday" carries a scene that is an eloquent reflection of this principle. Toward the end of the film the American football team are facing the game of their lives. It's the last quarter and Al Pacino in his role as coach gives the team talk. Eyeing each of the players he says with intensity (in vintage Pacino style!) that the game is like life. It is a game of inches. You fight for each inch toward the goal, and then most importantly: you hold onto that inch. Then you fight for another and then another. Eventually you reach the goal and you win the game.

Winning the game of life or losing the game of life occurs in pretty much the same way. It tends to occur inch by inch. Are you giving up inch by inch? Or do you advance inch by inch and not protect the advance? Either of these means losing. Or are you advancing inch by inch, protecting and cherishing the advance and finally getting to your goal, in this case a fulfilled and enriched life.

Some people tell me that their lives would be very different if they had chosen a different life partner/ moved to a different city, changed careers when an opportunity arose, retired early, had children, didn't have children, and so on and so forth. Most of us have some version of the big choices that we made or didn't make. And in most cases, we are deluding ourselves. Let us take an example of the life damaging relationship or marriage that lasts ten or fifteen years and has brought little but heartache.

As the disillusioned spouse talks, he/she describes the person as someone who has perhaps brought great difficulty or trouble into their lives. He speaks of the bad decision to marry. That may be the case but the problem was not that he/she married this person. That choice is simple. In most cases it is the culmination of many more subtle decisions. These smaller decisions often result from either not knowing how to make healthy choices, or denying the inner voice that is warning that those choices are leading to danger. In this example, I am assuming here, for the sake of the point, that the partnership was deeply flawed early on.

My work often involves hearing the history of relationships that have ended badly. In many cases I hear a whole series of little decisions. The choice one makes to ignore that little voice that said on the third date, 'she is very negative about her own family'. Maybe that voice was telling him that he should check to see what is truly behind the negativity. The choice to ignore his lack of attentiveness to her needs during lovemaking. Maybe that reflected a selfishness that continued to mark out the relationship during its lifetime. Or then again, the choice to cancel that trip with friends because the new relationship is in the way. Maybe that reflected an insecurity or jealousy that would lead to control and unhappiness later. The growing distance with friends because it doesn't suit a partner. These and many more are indicators that mean a certain sacrificing of important aspects of the self for the sake of a relationship. These choices to surrender important parts of one's identity for 'love' almost always lead to diminishment.

A useful metaphor here is that of the smoke alarm in your house. Imagine waking up in the middle of the night to the piercing sound of the smoke alarm going off. You clamber sleepily out of bed and reach up and turn it off. After all its very uncomfortable. Then you get back into bed, fall asleep and the house burns down. Many bad decisions are made by turning off the upset or discomfort caused by some observations about how something is affecting you. That, added then to some version of unrealistic optimism about how people might change, can lead to extraordinary costly outcomes.

One of the great challenges facing educating people is to teach the value of freedom and the danger of surrendering important aspects of one's personality for the safety of relationship. A great number of people give away their freedom in order to avoid aloneness. This is understandable. Being alone can be painful but it is a great error to trade that feeling for a disillusioned entrapment in a lonely relationship. Perhaps a deeper kind of loneliness is the surrender of hope that inheres many marriages. I see a lot of this in the work I do on a day to day basis. I listen and watch people recount the awful emptiness and sometimes terrible chronic distress of staying in a loveless marriage out of fear of economic struggle, isolation, judgement of others and fear for children's future. This is the prison that many people who gave insufficient value to their individual lives and attached themselves to another out of abdication or ignorance. When you reflect on the failure of the relationship, or the career, or the friendship it often becomes clear that there were many little choices and compromises that now appear to be adding up to the pattern that is at the heart of these losses. None of these choices in themselves are necessarily wrong or bad. Compromise, sensitivity to others, and negotiating are always a part of a good relationship. The crucial distinction is to know what to compromise on, what to negotiate on and when to surrender the ground. When the choices culminate in a big disaster then you didn't make the right choices. The best you can do now is learn to make better choices next time. All choice is relative to some outcome, and all behaviour is purposeful.

Becoming free means making choices that are clearly related to the outcome of the life that you seek. This means taking time to reflect on the choices you have made that have brought you to where you are now. It means becoming an aware person who knows how to make healthy choices (the inches) that add up to a healthy and fulfilling life.

We can now see that freedom is an absolute essential in determining how we live for good or ill. If we have no freedom then nothing we read about personal development is of value. Even for those who have strong religious convictions that demand surrender to God's will must acknowledge that you have to have the choice to surrender. Once you have made the choice to surrender your will to that of God's will as you understand it, you have chosen that path. And you can also choose to leave that path. Our first task then is to capture freedom and to enhance and expand it.

I have already alluded to the simplicity and naiveté that inheres in a lot of what is said about personal change. The key element in the illusion is that change is dramatic or sudden. In most cases it is not. A weekend seminar here, a self-help book there, a personal empowerment coaching session somewhere else does not add up to significant personal change. Each might help along the way, but the crucial ingredient in the recipe of change starts the day that you decide that you are going to become the manager of your life. This concept seems quite simple, and yet a great number of people live and die without ever realizing that their life is something that they must decide to own and take care of. Rather, they simply react to the circumstances around them and look to others for a plan for how to be. At no point do they realize that this will lead them to live a life determined by somebody or something else.

The decision to make your life a "work in progress" does not in itself make for change, rather it locates the source of change in yourself. You will notice the word 'become'. This is important because it communicates a process. Becoming your own life manager has two elements: (i) the allocation of the position at a point in time (I am now taking over as manager of my life), and, (ii) the rest of your life working at the job. Many walks of life reflect this simple but profound concept. The decision to marry someone is made on a certain day, the process of being married lasts for some until divorce. For others, those truly fortunate, it means a lifelong relationship that is good and fulfilling, and others, less fortunate, have a lifetime of chronic misery with each other, and the again for others a reasonable co-existence that keeps loneliness at bay but never provides true intimacy.

Deciding to take responsibility for your life, or for the more literary minded, the author of your life story, can have profound effects. One of these seems to be to be a subconscious shift in the way that you evaluate your world. Once you have taken on the position of managing your life the world seems to come into a different focus. You see things from the perspective of opportunities for your own development, and are less likely to waste time complaining and blaming others for the state of your life. When you meet good managers in other walks of life they tend to take responsibility rather than blame their staff. From McDonalds to Google good managers accept that the buck stops with them.

Another subtle change occurs in the way that you approach decisions. Once again, the world of commerce can be instructive. When you are a manager you bear greater responsibility so you make decisions more carefully. If you are a good manager you put the health of the organization first, so you don't react on impulse, you don't squander resources, and you don't jeopardize what you are responsible for. Equally, you may have to make tough decisions, to close certain outlets, to reschedule loans, to drop products that are no longer viable, even if you are sentimentally attached to them. Managing your life carries the same principles. An effective life manager makes informed decisions to enhance and build the strength and quality of his/her life.

Some of the other principles outlined below can be of help in become an effective manager of your own life.

Accept that not choosing is a choice

One of the great cop-outs in life is to avoid making choices. Realizing that not choosing is a choice prevents us from allowing ourselves to escape from personal responsibility. Those of us who avoid decisions are often driven by fear. If you don't hang your colours to the mast then you cannot be targeted. Not choosing saves us from risk. For some the risk of making a mistake is so great that they feel paralyzed. They stand immobile like Hobson's donkey between two bales of hay. For some it is the fear of failure that prevents them, for others it is the fear that there are better opportunities over the next hill, so they spend their lives climbing and never stop to experience the view.

One way that a person can avoid making choices is to let others be their guide for how to live. This is what 19th century philosopher Nietzsche calls the mentality of the herd. A useful illustration can be gained by watching sheep. A friend of mine once noted that sheep only become really stupid when they are separated from the flock. They have no guiding principles of their own and thus follow the leader, who also generally has no idea where she is heading. Sheep are programmed genetically to operate as a flock. This has a protective function as it provides some safety for when the wolf comes. If you are in a flock of a hundred sheep then the odds are you will not be eaten. If you leave the flock it is a certainty that you will be.

An interesting feature of being human is that we can revert to lower levels of functioning in the face of adversity. We all have a sheep brain that operates beneath the cerebral cortex. So, it is relatively easy for us to reduce our functioning to the level of a sheep for a period of time. It is however far more serious when we do it for our whole life. Fear of being eaten by the metaphorical wolf of social rejection, or the pain of failure, or of being noticed as standing out from the herd can be very frightening for some. Adolescence is a good case in point. The paradox of young people striking out to assert their individuality and difference from their parents is rather humorously undone when you see groups of these adolescents all wearing the same clothes and hairstyles. Their fear graduated from being too like their parents to being afraid of being unlike their peers.

Some of us never really resolve this conundrum. How to risk being yourself if it means being different from others. The temptation is to take your lead for how to live by not making any choices of your own, with the exception of choosing to not choose. Simply follow the lead of others in all the major aspects of life, the steady job, the right car, the appropriate clothes, membership of the right clubs, mass on Sundays, and so on and so forth.

Not choosing is a betrayal of your life. It is seductive and safe but often leads ultimately to bitterness and disappointment. If you are consistently avoiding life decisions you are saving up a store of disillusionment that will eventually catch up with you. It seems to be almost a life law that abdication of decisions does not go unpunished. And I dread to see the pain that some people face in their later years when they realize that a lifetime of avoidance has simply led them to being unable to avoid the greatest of all failures, a wasted life. Not choosing is a choice, and it is one that can carry a horrendous price. Perhaps the most eloquent description of this problem is that given to us by Danish philosopher Soren Kierkegaard. All of a hundred and seventy years ago he mapped out a most wonderful description of how the human being copes with the extraordinary challenge of being alive and self-aware. He writes *" man...his self or he himself is a something with 'the other' in the compass of the temporal and the worldly....Thus the self coheres immediately with 'the other' wishing, desiring, enjoying, etc but passively... he manages to imitate the other men, noting how they manage to live, and so he too lives after a sort. In Christendom he too is a Christian, goes to church every Sunday, hears and understands the Parson, yea they understand each other; he dies and the parson introduces* *him into eternity for the price of $10—but a self he was not, and a self he did not become ...for the immediate man does not recognise his self.. He recognises himself only by his dress...he recognises that he has a self only by externals"*

One important consideration needs to be addressed here. In speaking of the role that fear plays in preventing people from making choices to leave situations, to embark on new projects or to risk failure, we may minimise the paralysing power that fear can be. One particular type of fear is the fear that is placed in the heart of the victim of trauma. Traumatised people are not simply afraid to take risks. They are sometimes overwhelmed.

It is unfair to suggest that their paralysis in the face of that which they fear is something that they can simply overcome with a bracing of themselves or a firm resolution. "Feel the fear and do it anyway" may sometimes be a useful principle, but once again there are many situations when it is folly to follow it. When faced with crippling fear it is important to reach out for help. One of the central tasks of counselling and psychotherapy is to help people deal with fear. There are many forms of early life trauma that can have profound effects on freedom in later life. Sometimes the best a person can do is to use their freedom to choose by taking an initial step of getting help. I have discussed this issue in detail in an earlier book: Healing the Hurts of Childhood" That may be a useful resource for those who feel that their fear is overwhelming. It is also a truism that we are not islands and it is often a crucial aspect of making changes to enlist the support of true friends, support groups or professional guides.

Take responsibility for where you are now

Many years ago I wrote "The only point we can start at in our lives is the point we are at. If we see life and growth as a journey we may want to be in a different place along the road. We will not get to that place, however, until we accept and recognise, however painful it is, just where we are now. Rather we will spend our time and energy in fantasy, dreaming and wishing about how things could be different only to wake up a year or many years later in exactly the same place" (Children under the Influence. 1993. p.80).

As I review these words written decades ago, I have an opportunity to review many of the changes and developments in my own life since then. Decades on, I am a wiser man. I have had a share of disasters; I have made some bad errors of judgement that led to much distress and suffering. I have also created some things of which I am proud. I am far more aware of who I am and continue to learn and grow in my life. The principle of starting from where you are works: I know this because I can track the course of these three decades and see that there is a continual steady progression. The journey has been erratic at times but the direction is always there, it is a direction that is determined by my chosen life purpose.

To expand your sense of freedom you need to acknowledge to yourself where you are now. Philosopher Martin Heidegger's philosophy is useful here. At any one point in your life you are at a point between your past and your future. This is a very powerful image. The future you create will be tomorrow's past. At each point you are also bringing your past with you in the form of memory and experience. There is no 'now' that is not full of you. It is important here to digress a little and explore some of the inaccurate material out there on this topic. You cannot separate yourself from your past because your very identity is constructed from it and you cannot jettison it. There are a variety of diseases that afflicts some people who lose their memory. Alzheimer's is one such disease and the results are heartrending. When a person loses their past by virtue of losing their memory, they lose the significance of all their relationships with people, as well as the skills and learning that have helped them construct their lives. They become shells. Only a crazy person would suggest that trying to live without a past is a form of mental health. Another, rarer phenomenon is that of traumatic amnesia usually as a result of brain injury. The bestselling novel 'The Housekeeper and the Professor' is a beautifully crafted story that so well describes the importance of memory to our sense of identity.

Equally in some of the current self-help writings we are told that there is no future. Wrong again, there are many possible futures but they are always in the process of creation. So, as we stand at that nodal point between the past that defines so much of our identity and the future that we are always oriented toward, we carry the sculpting tool of freedom, to make the future from that past. That is the essence of human freedom. And again, a reminder, it is a freedom within limitations. As you read this you are at that nodal point and the question and challenge here is what kind of a future you are going to create.

Let us imagine a man called John Everyman as he examines his position at the nodal point. He might describe it thus: I am John Everyman, I am 46 years old. I live with my wife of 22 years. I am content with her. I dislike my job as a sales manager in the supermarket but feel I have no option for change. I have three children, Peter a boy of 17 who I fight with and two girls, Laura who is 20 and who I feel close to, and Isabel 18 who I cannot seem to communicate with. I am financially secure but bored in my life. I watch too much television and dream of building a boat in my spare time. I am lazy and physically unfit but am not too worried about it.

In terms of the task of creating his future there is much in the above that can help John to plan some changes. He may or may not take up this challenge but at least he knows where he is at a particular moment in time. This is the snapshot. If, in a year's time, he is still in the same job, has a year's more television watched and is a few pounds heavier, is further alienated from his daughter and estranged from his son, he will at least know that the direction towards stagnation and boredom is progressing nicely! On the other hand, he may have started lessons on boat building and enjoying the company of others similarly involved.

He may have engaged in understanding some of the problems with communicating with his daughter and he may even have set out on a different career path.

The Sculpting Tool of Freedom

If we cannot, and should not, jettison our past, then what should we do with it. We use it to help us understand those aspects that we wish to retain and expand, and those we wish to diminish and disarm. We can also gain insight into the misconceptions that led us to make unwise decisions and we can reorient ourselves. On this point I remember a television interview with the singer/songwriter Sting. During the interview he was challenged by the interview with regard to a particular topic (I can't remember it specifically but I think it was a political issue). The interviewer exclaimed, "but this is a very different view than the one you held in our last interview two years ago". "Yes", replied Sting, "I changed my mind since then. That is what intelligent people do"! In other words, intelligent people learn from their experiences and thus can change their minds and do things differently. Another unfortunate mantra in a lot of self-help literature is that, in life there are no mistakes, only lessons. Wrong again. A lesson is a mistake you learn from, and thus avoid repeating. The important thing is that our future should contain new mistakes (because you are going to make them) not a repeat of the old ones. Or more simply, the trick is to turn our mistakes into lessons. That is one of the keys to wisdom.

If you do not reflect on and analyse your past then you will end up making the same mistakes because you will not have new knowledge to work with. Your past is a treasure trove of information and experience (knowledge) that can help you construct a future that is worthwhile. It is from the present that you can construct a new past (the one you will reflect on in the future). This is the true power of now. Your current past may, on reflection, contain too much of one set of experiences, such as living too much for others expectations, squandering financial resources, living a boring and unfulfilled career, or on the other hand, it may not reflect enough of other experiences that are important for a fulfilling life. Maybe for you this means, better sex, closer communication with your children, a deeper sense of achievement. If your reflection/examination of your past reveals these issues, then you are challenged to begin a process whereby your new past will contain less of the former and more of the latter. Sounds simple and yet there are many pitfalls. This is the subject of the next chapter.

Summary

Your thoughts do affect your feelings and can help you to clarify some aspects of your life. They also send messages to your unconscious that can gradually sway your priorities. They do not cure diseases, make you rich, or make you lose weight. They have almost no impact on any external reality. That only happens when you DO something different in response to your thinking. Thinking, in itself, does not make it so.

This chapter explored the nature of freedom and its role in the creation of meaning. It suggested that freedom is a human capability that can be enhanced and strengthened with practice. It also suggested that we can use whatever freedom we have to enslave ourselves. And the resulting outcome of years of such small choices can lead to an almost complete entrapment. The progressive use of freedom to gradually increase our power over our lives is the authentic way forward. This is a gradual process involving careful consideration of the consequences of the decisions we make. It involves recognising that at every point in our lives we are standing between the past that is full of our experience and the future which we have yet to create. What we do in each of these moments ends up being the very definition of our being in the world. The true power of now lies in this incredible challenge. At each point we are presented with the possibility of taking a step. There are an infinite number of points on the compass, so we must get some guiding principle to use to help us take that step. That guiding principle comes from the map we create for our future. The next chapter discusses how we go about mapping out the future that we wish to create.

Chapter 4.
Authentic Life Purpose

He who has a why to live can bear almost any how.
Friedrich Nietzsche

Introduction.

Thus far we have discussed several of the essential elements in living authentically. These are a caring and respectful attitude to the self, distinguishing your true self from your constructed self, as well as developing and expanding one's sense of freedom. These can be seen as a foundation upon which to build the structure of a life. That structure can be understood can consisting of three different interconnected aspects, what we create, what we experience, and our relationships.

Human beings are creatures of meaning. We look for patterns in our surroundings, and we seek to make sense of random events. It is a frightening and despairing thought to consider life as an absurd and meaningless venture that for most of us lasts a few decades. Our resistance to such despair is important for our well-being. And thus, it is important to search for a way to live that gives us a sense of meaning and purpose.

One branch of psychotherapy 'Logotherapy' was developed with this core element of human functioning in mind. Based on his experience as a prisoner in Auschwitz, psychiatrist Victor Frankl set out to show that every human being carries within what he calls a meaning vacuum. Unless we fill that vacuum with something that gives us meaning in life, we will live lives of desperation, marked out by addiction, mental illness, despair, anxiety and depression. And when faced with adversity there will not be the courage and resilience that comes from a strong sense of meaning to help us survive. In our Western societies we need such reassurance now more than ever as our dalliance with raw capitalism failed and has left many stranded on the shores of unemployment, poverty, debt and economic strife. Because a sense of meaning is so important for human happiness, societies generally have offered readymade sources for it members. Like all such systems, they have the quality of being readily accessible. The downside being that they provide a readymade source of meaning and in doing so make it easy for an individual to avoid the task of carving out his or her own source of meaning. In Nietzsche's inimitable words: *"The individual has always had to struggle to keep from being overwhelmed by the tribe. If you try it, you will be lonely often, and sometimes frightened. But no price is too high to pay for the privilege of owning yourself."* Before examining how to go about cultivating a personal source of meaning it is important to present the more common sources that are provided by ones social and cultural context.

Sources of Meaning
Religion

The tremendous importance of having a sense of meaning is easily recognised in the universal presence of religion throughout human history. My discussion here will be brief for the requirements of this book. I have explored this topic in more detail in a different work entitled "Misled? How Ideology Captures your Mind". Different cultures reflect very different religious ideas and ideologies. Over the centuries many changes occur, mainly from religions populated by somewhat limited and unpredictable gods such as those in the early Greek mythologies as well as more currently in the Hindu tradition. More recent history has seen a movement toward the more modern monotheistic character (one almighty God) that now is central to the three great religious movements of Western culture: Judaism, Christianity and Islam.

In general, the role that religion has played in human history has been to assuage the fears and doubts about the triviality of our existence in this world. Its whole significance has been to help people feel that their lives are following some divine purpose, and to comfort us as we face the end of life with a belief in the hereafter. All religious systems have these key elements. Some however have an additional concern, that of providing a set of moral imperatives that are important in terms of how we should live, and determining what happens to us after we die. For many people then religious belief is their main source of meaning in life. Their suffering, should it occur, can be understood as something to be endured as given by God, or at least an opportunity to increase faith and resilience. Happiness and joyful experience can also be understood as gifts given by the creator, perhaps as a reward for good deeds, or simply as an act of his/her beneficence.

It is thus an option for any person to use religious belief as a source of meaning. This is a choice. It causes a bit of distress to zealous believers in a religion that religious belief should be seen as a choice, because by definition, in their view, religion is a matter of truth. And history tells us that human beings have a peculiar penchant for killing each other in great numbers (often with a dose of torture as a precursor) precisely over the matter of who holds the true faith and who is the heretic/infidel. Most people are of the view, for example, that we don't or shouldn't have a choice to believe whether or not the earth is round. And yet there are some people who still believe that the earth is flat. In this belief they are mistaken. Religious truths are seen in a similar context, those who hold such true beliefs are saved, those who contradict them, or refuse to accept, are damned, at least in some shape of form. And then again there are those who posit the notion that any belief in religious doctrine is a mistake.

In the main however, people argue about which religious doctrine or claims are true and which are not true. God, by any definition, cannot be self-contradictory so most of the beliefs about the nature of God must be mistaken, because so many religious systems hold divergent views of God. These are some of the conundrums and difficulties that face any person who wishes to hold a mature faith, but there are many ways these can be resolved, and that too is a personal choice. This question is beyond the task of this book.

Cultivating faith in a religious system is therefore one possibility for those who wish to find meaning for their lives. Choosing or losing a religion or a form of worship is of course fraught with certain dangers. I have a few suggestions with regard to how to choose a religious belief while maintaining authenticity. Those systems that carry within them a denigration of others who do not share the same beliefs are intrinsically evil. The study of human evil tells us that one element in evil systems is reducing the dignity or value of other people based purely on their culture or beliefs. It is best to avoid any religious ideology that denigrates or reduces the dignity of others.

Systems that prize or champion suffering in the present for rewards in the afterlife are also suspect. No system that makes a virtue out of suffering is worthy of consideration. Suffering is not, in itself, a virtue. Most suffering is avoidable, and is a product of bad decisions, cruelty on the part of those in power, lack of awareness, ignorance, low self-worth and a negative and pessimistic view of life. Some suffering is unavoidable, and the unfairness of life is that some individuals are burdened with a great deal of unavoidable suffering. The virtue in suffering, if any, can be found in the courage, stoicism and resilience that is reflected in some of those individuals who are brave and humane in spite of it. If one's religious belief sustains a person through dark times, without making a virtue of such dark times then it offers something really worthwhile. In this regard I am sympathetic to Somerset Maugham's adage that "suffering does not ennoble the character, happiness sometimes does".

Religious systems that promote a god that is less humane than your average mature human are also suspect. I find it interesting that some people believe in and worship a God who is like an omnipotent toddler. Toddlers are, in general, impulsive, lacking in self-control, over-reactive and don't know their own destructive power. They have temper tantrums when they don't get the attention they need. Some people live in fear of a God who will kill people, or punish them for eternity for not believing in him!! I find this extraordinary. Recently I watched an excerpt from a lecture delivered by a fundamentalist teacher from a particular faith to a group of philosophy students. One student had the temerity to ask about the problem of theodicy (the question of how could a good god allow evil in the world). The lecturer lost his temper and after mocking the study of philosophy he said to the student "the important question is why the Lord does not kill you in your bed". Phew!

Those who mock or denigrate religious belief tend to do so on the basis that such beliefs are delusional and without merit. Rationalists such as Richard Dawkins, Christopher Hitchens, and Jonathan Singer make strong arguments that they believe show that most of what was originally credited to God is now recognised as resulting from naturally occurring phenomena. The old classic example is worth noting that thunder is not the angry exclamations of god, it is the explosive noise of a lightning strike. What is often missed in these arguments is the point that religious experience is not a matter of scientific fact. I once read a lovely expression to the effect that scientific rationalism applied to religious experience is akin to explaining a violin concerto as a matter of someone dragging the hair of a horse over the guts of a cat! (in earlier days before synthetic production, violin strings were made from cat gut, and the bow was constructed from horse hair).

I am partial to religious faiths that talk of loving God who sends his angels to watch over and protect people. I am also partial to the notion that there is some form of justice in the world and that cruel and evil acts do not go without sanction, either here or in the afterlife. Of course, I cannot prove any of this, nor can I disprove it. And I am not silly enough to believe that my choice to believe will change any external reality. There is either a God (or gods) or there isn't. The nature of that God if he /she exists is also not simply a product of my/

your belief. Religious belief also usually involves rituals and practices such as prayer and devotional activities. These often occur in a group setting and thus help to bind people together in community. All of these can have positive and comforting effects. If you want to use a religious framework for a sense of meaning and purpose it is essential that you choose carefully. Only embrace those elements that will offer you meaning without corrupting your morals or teaching you to persecute, mistreat or diminish yourself or others.

Sport

Renowned football coach Bill Shankly is famous for his quotation "Some people believe football is a matter of life and death, I am very disappointed with that attitude. I can assure you it is much, much more important than that." It may seem strange to place sport in the same section as a discussion of religion. However, it is probably the activity along with religion that provides millions of people with a sense of meaning. I am not here discussing people who play sport. That is a hobby/career that provides a healthy expression of physical and mental prowess. Here I am discussing that loyalty and identification with a club or team. It plays such a massive role in some people's lives that any discussion of meaning that leaves it out would be barren indeed.

I try to imagine what would happen if the English Premiership and the GAA championship was dismantled here in Ireland. Monday morning on all the factory floors, supermarkets, offices, construction sites would become silent. Sport is a strong source of meaning because it comes from an emotional attachment to a club, or team. The intensities of this attachment can run very deep. They tell us that as human beings we need to find something bigger that ourselves to identify with. In this sense it is a tribal phenomenon. It has very little to do with athleticism. I smile when I see a grossly overweight football fan bursting the seams of his team's football jersey, to all external observers a clear example of ill health, bad diet and no exercise. His devotion is less to do with the athleticism of the game and more to do with his sense of belonging and a focus for his conversations and connection to something greater than himself: i.e. his club.

Yesterday, I had a great conversation with a client who returned for a review session some time after completing a course of sessions with me. He had lived and breathed for his devotion to a Premier League soccer team. He began that devotion as a child and now at forty yrs. old he invested money in season tickets, travel to the UK and all the attendant details. His online friends were in regular contact with him around all the issues arising with the team. This was probably his most identifiable source of meaning. As a result of our work together he was able to gain awareness into how little self-esteem and confidence he had. Equally, he was able to get the courage to take on a college foundation course that would allow him access to third level education. I encouraged this course for him because I could see that he had lost his way very early in life and had great potential for more satisfying work particularly in the area of care. His personality, intelligence level and social skills were all there but with no confidence, no focus, and no qualifications or training he would not be able to actualise these elements of his true self in a productive and fulfilling way.

As we spoke he described all the fears, anxieties and worries that attended his first few days at his course. Having been ridiculed and abandoned as a young teenager in school he was naturally full of trepidation even walking into a college, a place where he felt he had no right to be. After a month all this began to change, and now he describes the feeling of exhilaration and confidence growing each day that he attends. It is joyful for me to see this transformation. In the context of this conversation about change he mentions in passing that he has almost lost all interest in his soccer team. He himself is almost shocked at how it just disappeared from his consciousness. It no longer has any meaning for him.

This had happened gradually and with no real attention to this part of his life. As he progressed in his own life evaluation, setting some new goals, gaining some confidence and productive interests as well as overcoming some crippling self-doubt and low self-esteem, what was really a fanatical connection to the soccer club just gradually died. This does not mean that enjoying sports and having an affinity to a team is a negative thing. I very much enjoy my own loyalty to a football club and just as enthusiastically shout at the screen when they play badly and can jump for joy when they score. This activity only becomes a problem when it replaces a deeper spiritual need for meaning.

Over a hundred years ago Karl Marx described religion as "the opium of the people". By this he meant that religion provides a sedative to the human spirit, deadening its reaction to what he observed to be the patent inequalities in society, the alienation of most workers from the means of production and the widespread exploitation of the productive energies of people. In the current age, now a secular one with a post Christian ethos, it could easily be argued that tribal allegiance to football clubs is a new form of existential opium.

Children

Perhaps the most common source of meaning for people in all walks of life is that of having children. Most people who bring children into the world tend to define a large part of their sense of meaning in life in terms of their children's' welfare and wellbeing. Although some go about the task of parenting in ways that can cause a lot of difficulty and hardship for their offspring, they still see their role as parents as a source of meaning and purpose for their lives. Victor Frankl, author of the classic "Man's Search for Meaning" counsels against seeing our children as a source of meaning. He believes that reproducing ourselves cannot in itself be seen as meaningful. Our own lives must have meaning if we are to assume that having children brings meaning. That, to me seems a rather academic point, and doesn't seem to take into account the extraordinary bonds of love, sacrifice and attachment that for most people, inheres in the experience of being a parent. That said, it should also be mentioned that there a significant number of people who choose to bring children into the world whose lives would be better had they not done so. Some find the task of parenthood too difficult, and for some it is a very damaging and life constricting. They lose the energy and the hope that they could have had for other projects in the mistaken belief that having children is a necessary or essential part of fulfilled adulthood. Having children therefore is a choice that traps and disempowers the lives of some people. This is particularly so in today's world of nuclear families. The family unit consists of two parents, or the growing reality of single parents sharing parenting in different locations, separated from any communal involvement. This type of family structure leaves the parents and the children exposed to risks when the parents are not mature or well enough to rear children on their own.

This point is often lost amidst the general fiction that bringing up children is always a worthwhile and noble task. Not enough is said on behalf of those parents who go through hell trying as best they can to deliver their children into adulthood healthy in mind and body only to fail catastrophically. I have seen people whose lives have been laid waste by their children. Recent generations, nourished on the diet of popular psychology, has seen the blame for all tribulation and difficulty in the lives of children, too easily foisted on parents. Having children is a risk. It can ruin your life. The novel "We need to talk about Kevin" is a wonderfully crafted work that captures many aspects of the real-life experience encountered by people who have their spirits broken by their children. However, with that caveat in mind it can be said that for most people the joy and deep fulfilment that comes with being a parent outweighs the struggle and tribulations that go with that challenge.

Work

Having children is perhaps the most obvious form of creating something to give life meaning. It is however only one such example. Another source of meaning is that of work, or gainful employment. This is a source of meaning that is, in fact, quite rare in a developed capitalist economy. One of Karl Marx's key insights is that capitalism almost always leads to a type of alienation between the worker and work. The worker becomes a means of production, a link in a chain, a cog in the machine. The work itself, for the majority, has no meaning except as a way of getting money. Thus, the riveter in the shipyard, the checkout girl in the supermarket, the butcher in the meat factory rarely find meaning in the tasks that use up their productive energy.

When it comes to the issue of work as a source of meaning it is therefore important to distinguish between productivity and creativity. In order to fulfil our responsibilities to take care of ourselves and those who depend on us, most people must find a source of income. Unfortunately, it is the lot of most people that their productive lives, do not really give them a sense of meaning. Almost all of us can remember sitting in school in front of a burnt-out shell of a person who should never have been a teacher. The men who collect my rubbish at six in the morning on wet and freezing West of Ireland mornings are unlikely to see their job as creative or meaningful. They do it to earn a crust and feed their families. An excellent exploration of this theme is found in the movie "About Schmidt" One of my favourite actors, Jack Nicholson captures the alienation and ennui of the insurance salesman main character. The film opens as he sits waiting in his empty office, on his last day at work while the clock ticks down to 5pm. The speech at his retirement party is an achingly moving summary of a lifetime of productive energy spent at a job that has no meaning for the unfortunate Schmidt. The remainder of the film is a hilariously dark exploration of the man's search for something to be proud of, to redeem something of worth for his life.

It is important therefore to recognise that the activities that give meaning sometimes must take place outside the hours that are spent in productive labour. That is a legacy of modern life. Capitalism as an economic system has the downside that most workers find no meaning in their work. They can however earn money, some of which can be invested in activities that lead to a sense of meaning. In turn, it is possible to work toward finding a way to connect productivity and meaning. Some of the most fulfilled people in the world are those that have managed to work at something that gives their lives a sense of meaning. This is a great prize and one worth pursuing.

These four areas: religion, sport, children and work are common sources of meaning for people. They are, to a large extent, the meaning menu on the table of Western society. The other major pillar being relationships which I will discuss in more detail in the chapter following.

Accumulating wealth and status.

There is a meaning vacuum in our souls, and we can end up filling it with something hollow and counterfeit because we do not know how else to deal with it. Perhaps the best example of this folly is presented in the drive to fill a life with the pursuit of wealth. There is nothing intrinsically wrong or dysfunctional about wanting to have wealth. Money often brings new possibilities, as well as the power to add new experiences and elements to a life. A nicer house, a better car, good food, better medical care and so on and so forth. It is however a great folly to think that money itself has any 'meaning' quality. The meaning quality lies in the person who has the money, and the money allows the actualisation of that meaning. Thus, a person with aesthetic flair and taste, who becomes wealthy, will be able to afford to decorate tastefully and perhaps buy artefacts that bring joy to the eye. Most of us can recall seeing the results of someone having lots of money and no taste. A big 'white elephant' of a house adorned with expensive bling and crass stands as a tribute to money without taste. A wealthy person with idealism and concern for the care of others and the environment may set up a charity that brings great fulfilment and satisfactions. Then again there is the phenomenon of lives ruined by the sudden enrichment through lottery winning because they cannot cope with the instant access to all kinds of products and lifestyle opportunities without the spiritual depth required to handle all the possibilities for excess.

Adding money to a life does not necessarily add meaning, and in many instances material wealth goes hand in hand with spiritual poverty. This is because the pursuit of wealth for its own sake often comes at the cost of surrendering or losing the very qualities required for authentic living. This is a principle referred to in the holy writ when Jesus explains by way of parable that it is easier for a camel to get through the eye of a needle that for a rich man to get to the kingdom of heaven. This is somewhat different from those who become 'accidentally' wealthy in virtue of some creative pursuit. Some musicians, writers, dancers and even footballers, gain their wealth, not purely by pursuing their craft, but because that craft, fortunately for them, becomes rewarded (often to absurd levels) by people who see the opportunity to create wealth by selling the enjoyment and entertainment to a wide audience. Such creative souls would be pursuing their craft even in the maw of poverty, and many of the greatest artists have spent decades in the shadows, living in poverty and eking out a subsistence living.

Discovering an Authentic Sense of Meaning.

One of the great conundrums about this subject is whether or not our lives have an intrinsic meaning. This alludes to the question of whether our lives have some purpose outside of that which we give it. On a personal level, if Michael Hardiman did not become a psychologist and work as a counsellor/educator, would he have failed in his given purpose in life. My answer to this question is that I do not believe that I would have failed some universal law or God appointed task had I become a plumber or an astrophysicist. I would have failed to honour my true self's calling, and that for me is the key to the meaning of our lives. From a religious point of view, it can be argued that the calling of the true self is in fact the call of God or the Universe. James Hillman helpfully clarifies the point by telling us that the oak tree is in the acorn. Our meaning is in the true self, and finding and actualising that meaning is one of the great life tasks, along with the discovery of authentic love. The following is some guidance of how to discovery that meaning.

Here's a useful question. When it comes time for you to die, what do you want to leave behind in the world that is there because you made it? Is it a beautiful garden? Is it a house that contained love and laughter? Is it an industry or workshop that provides a livelihood for people? How about a book that entertained? Maybe a role on stage that brought relief and fun. Is it a group of people who are educated because you taught them? Maybe a family that is secure and happy! Or then again paintings that evokes a sense of beauty or even puzzlement among those who look at it. Perhaps children that have a treasure chest of memories of you? People who you cared for when they were hurt or lost? Animals whose lives were safe and well cared for? And so on and so forth. Ralph Waldo Emerson said it well in his short verse that *"To leave the world a bit better, whether by a healthy child, a garden patch, or a redeemed social condition; to know that even one life has breathed easier because you have lived — that is to have succeeded."* There are hundreds of possibilities, some are modest, some are exceptional, but most importantly, they are personal. This first exercise in the search for meaning then is one of inquiry.

For most people who live fulfilled and essentially happy lives they have a combination of satisfying and fulfilling activities. In that regard, life is less like the box of chocolates made famous by Forrest Gump, and more like baking a cake. You have to have certain ingredients in right amounts for it to work. There may be one or two primary purposeful projects, family, work and the like, with other less dominant but equally important activities that bring joy and laughter. The important part here is that each element is subjectively meaningful, that means that they feel a sense of meaning in the engagement. The following is a description of how to use our faculties so as to develop a life design to incorporate a deep sense of meaning.

Reflective Living

I want to use two metaphors here that may help guide towards self-reflection and awareness. The first is that of the dolphin. When we think about dolphins several things come to mind. They are graceful intelligent creatures whose lives are essentially spent swimming around doing dolphin things. They search for food, pursue their sex lives, look after their young and watch out for sharks. While they do all that they also communicate with each other and play as much as they can. They are thus immersed in dolphin life. This immersion in their life task is very like what Heidegger describes as the way that most humans live. For him the central notion that explains how we live is the notion of "care". We are 'concernfully' engaged in living and much of the time this is done without much reflection on the temporal nature of our lives. Dolphins interrupt their activities regularly to come to the surface for air. Reflective living can be compared to this activity. It means leaving the day to day 'busyness' of life now and then to take time for reflection.

Another metaphor that is useful is to consider life as a journey through a forest. Imagine that you have a task to reach the foot of a particular mountain that is surrounded by forest. As you travel along you will need to climb a tree so as to readjust your direction. If you do not do that then you will walk around in circles and find yourself consistently back where you started. How this happens is also of interest. In general, people are right-handed or left-handed (a few are ambidextrous). This means that there is a slight preference or dominance for one side of our bodies. When we set out on a trek for which we have few signposts or direction markers: (a desert, snow plains or forest/jungle for example), there will be a gradual tendency to move toward our dominant side. Even though our perception is that we are going in a straight line we are in fact going in a circle. Similarly, we have psychological preferences that are often unconscious, that are developed over time as a result of our formative experiences in our youth. These are what might be called default setting in our minds. Sometimes they will lead us away from our intended purpose if we do not consistently check our direction. Climbing a tree in the forest at regular intervals helps to keep us on the right track. This is the metaphor for taking time to reflect and check in with ourselves to see if we are reaching our goals.

The reader will notice here that living in the now is being described in terms of reflection on the past and orientation towards the future. This differs from the problem that many people encounter when they live *in* the past, or live *in* the future. In the former, one's energy is spent in futile regret or in the latter, optimistic fantasy /painful worry. These cause a person to lose the importance of the 'now'. Some writers have suggested that the way to avoid these futile ways of living is to replace it with 'living in the now'. This approach is however very suspect. Any system of thought that recommends that we jettison memory and future orientation and simply live in the now, is in fact recommending, that we no longer live in a fully human way. Rather, it is living more like an ox.

I enjoy watching nature programs. The wildebeest is a good example of a creature that lives only in the now. Its nose is almost permanently in the grass. Every now and then it takes off at the sight, sound, or smell of the approaching lion. Otherwise it seems to have no worries. It doesn't lift its head to appreciate the wonder of its existence, and it does not have to cope with the transience of its life. It has no project except to live, eat, defecate, and look for sex, and reproduce. And that is very well and good for a wildebeest. As a human being however, your very identity is shaped by experiences, encounters with others and how you deal with them, as well as self-creation which is largely determined by what you learn from and do with these experiences. A critical step then in living in a fully human way means learning how to become reflective about your life, and active in making choices based on that reflection. I like Ayn Rand's description and challenge when she writes "to think is an act of choice. The key to human nature ....is the fact that man is a <u>being of volitional consciousness</u>. Reason does not work automatically, thinking is not a mechanical process, the connections of logic are not made by instinct. The function of your stomach, lungs or heart is automatic. The function of your mind is not" (p.1013 Underlines added.)

The choice then, is to live with a wildebeest consciousness, in the now, without using the aspects of consciousness that make us human, or, to live in awareness, consciously using those aspects of the human mind that define our human nature.

Three aspects of human consciousness are particularly relevant here: (i) reflection, (ii) perception, and (iii) projection. Reflection concerns our understanding of the past. We can look to past events and experiences and examine them from the standpoint of our present situation, along with all the learning and experiences that have intervened. We therefore have, through the power of reflection, the ability to come to terms with our history, sometimes it means acceptance, other times it means forgiveness, and then again at times it means letting go. We can use past experiences to help us avoid certain people, or certain situations that are bad for us. All of this is crucial to the task of building an authentic and fulfilling life.

Perception concerns our understanding of the present. The way that we perceive events has a great influence on how they affect us. One thing that marks out human consciousness is the variety of ways that a single event can be interpreted by different people. The old saw of the glass half empty or half full is a good case in point. Of particular relevance here is, psychologist Martin Seligman's discovery of the phenomenon he called "learned helplessness". His research would not be allowed today because it involved putting dogs in a situation where they were repeatedly given shocks. However, a brief description is useful here. The basic experiment involved putting dogs in a cage that had a dividing line in the middle. One side was electrified and the other safe. The dogs on the electrified side received shocks that they could avoid by jumping over the line to a safe side of the cage. Some of the dogs had originally been put in a situation where they could not escape shocks whereas others had the possibility to avoid shocks by pressing a panel. These dogs learned that they could avoid the shocks. The dogs that originally learned that they could avoid shocks jumped to the safe side, whereas those that had been put in a no escape situation earlier did not. They simply waited passively to experience the shock and did not try to escape. Some even stayed in the cage when the door was left open. This powerful experiment showed that dogs learned that they were helpless. And in being so they became lethargic and surrendered to their fate. Seligman and others have generalised this to human beings and developed a theory of depression from it. It has also been used as a part of understanding Post Traumatic Stress Disorder. Consequently, it can be concluded found that if human beings find themselves in difficult circumstances over which they have no power for change, they can develop a hopeless helpless attitude to their lives. When circumstances change they do not change this internal way of framing events and thus do not make any efforts to change even when they have the power to do so. In consequence they miss or avoid opportunities that could improve their lives.

Projection concerns our orientation toward a future. It makes use of a unique feature of the human mind, namely imagination. Human beings are able to create an internal picture in their mind that is not based on any particular condition of their lived experience. I can imagine what a unicorn is, even though no such animal exists. I do so by bringing together several images that I do know about, a horse and a horn, and *voila* I have a picture of a unicorn in my mind. Some people are much better at this than others but all people have some ability in terms of using imagination.

Living in a fully human way requires an active choice to engage each aspect of our human consciousness. To be free means working with these aspects of consciousness in order to create and direct our lives. I call this approach reflective living.

Reflective Meditation

A lot of self-help literature (specifically the mind-body-spirit category) suggests that a big problem with people in the West is that they think too much. This is due to the influence of Eastern mysticism that tends to see thinking as a rather dubious exercise. My experience, however, is the opposite. I am of the opinion that, in general, people think too little. Much is made, for example, of following your 'instinct' or 'gut feelings' when it comes to making choices. This is interesting because it underplays the importance of thinking and reasoning. A friend of mine recently challenged me about this notion explaining to me that he doesn't place much trust on his mind when it comes to making decisions. Rather he prefers to rely on experience and gut feelings. This however raises a very big philosophical question. Where do our gut feelings come from? The notion of 'gut feelings' comes from archaic notions of the body that are now discredited.

In fact, all our interpretations of reality are grounded in learning. Immanuel Kant, considered by many to be one the greatest of all philosophers, spent a major part of his life addressing the question, "how do the sensations we encounter through our engagement with the world become what we call experience"? I am reluctant to recommend his magnum opus "Critique of Pure Reason" because it is not for the faint hearted. However, a short summary here is useful. Essentially you have to do something with an event for it to be translated into experience. You have to process it in some way for it to become part of your life map. He outlined a series of categories that human beings use to turn events into experience. These are all functions of the mind and go to make up a large part of how we reason. Reasoning then is the human capacity to learn from events and sensations caused by our interaction in the world. Relying on gut feelings is simply a form of reasoning that gives primacy to the emotional feelings that are perceived to be part of an event or a choice. You cannot separate reasoning from decisions. You can simply reason that your feelings rather than logic, for example, are the more important elements in deciding what to do.

You have probably noticed by now that I have a strong tendency to highly value thinking as an essential part of a full life. Those familiar with Descartes and other philosophers will realise that they used meditation as a form of focused thinking on a particular subject. That is the way that I am using it here. Reflective meditation is an exercise that involves focusing your mind, or more specifically, your reasoning powers, on the issue of where you are in your life at present and how well you are proceeding in your pursuit of your life tasks. Two human faculties are absolutely critical in this process. These are memory and imagination. You will recall the previous chapter where Heidegger's concept of the nodal point between the past and the future was considered. Let us add into that picture the use of memory and imagination. Memory is the faculty that relates us to past experience. Heidegger believes that remembering always has the character of "making-present of something which has been, something I experienced at the time...simply recalling something is not a remembering. A making-present is a remembering, only when I make something present as something I experienced at that time".

It might be useful here to play with the word 'remember' in order to fully clarify this point. There is an ancient use of the word "member". In the middle ages, doctors referred to the organs of the body as "members". We can use this to imagine that "re-membering" is about bringing an event/experience from our past to life: to add again the living organs of its nature, all the sounds, feelings, sights, and smells that it evoked at the time, to make it come alive again in our minds. With this conception of memory as the making-present of experiences:

good and bad, beautiful and ugly, gives a person their sense of unique identity, and perhaps an orientation toward a future where new memories will be created.

It is relevant to note that psychologists working with the elderly suggest that a key element of gracious and peaceful aging is the accumulation of memories that come to be 'made-present'. These provide consolation and sense of dignity for a life well lived. Memory then is not simply a recollection of information; it is not like picking up a file from the desk of the past and looking at it. Rather, it is a state of consciousness that connects us, in real time, to the emotional significance of events that we have been through. When we use our memory in this way, we gather insight that helps us to answer the question, what do I want my life task to be. What do I want to create, and what kind of relationships do I want to share myself in. The other faculty we have to work with is that of imagination. If memory is the faculty of making the past present to us, then imagination can be considered the faculty that brings the future into the present. Much has been written in the self-help literature of a version of imagination under the term 'visualisation'. I think this is a very limited understanding of the concept. Here I want to use Jean Paul Sartre's insight into the subject. He argues that what we refer to as imagination is better understood as 'imaging consciousness'. This term carries within it a central philosophical notion of intentionality. It is active, and refers to bringing our consciousness to bear in an intentional way toward possibility. It also opens our consciousness to a scene that is not simply visual. Our imaging consciousness brings all our senses to bear on the events/experiences that we intend for ourselves. We can transport ourselves into the later acts in the play of our lives, ones we have yet to create. When we combine these two faculties to address the project of choosing life tasks we use the power of our consciousness to make present those experiences that carry meaning from our past and project them forward into our future. To do this effectively means taking time to meditate on our lives.

As you combine these in reflective meditation you may find that two or three themes emerge consistently that are of significant importance. These can become the central themes of your life project in terms of what you want to create. When you see these more clearly you will have discovered a direction and you can set out along the path of meaning. Now we must return to the caution that is a constant feature of my writing. Stay away from unrealistic or impossible day-dreams. Every theme is just that. It waits to be actualised by you through your choices and dedication of your resources. There are many variations as to how a theme can be actualised. Someone who wants to look back at life and see a set of people who were touched and helped can actualise this in a variety of ways. The core value of care can be expressed by becoming a world-renowned brain surgeon on one hand, or someone who visits a lonely elderly person in a care facility on the other. The only difference is one of skill, education, opportunity. So, once you discover the themes then you can look at the resources in time, effort, finance and talent that you have to offer. Don't believe that you can be anything you want to be. You can't. Rather be the best you can be and point yourself in the direction of the core values that emerge from this exercise.

What Experiences to Enjoy

It is a truism that many of our most joyful experiences occur when we are not looking for them. More often they occur as a consequence of some other activity. In terms of what is discussed so far it can be said that following your life task will often bring experiences of deep satisfaction and fulfilment. There is however an additional piece. This involves using your resources to pursue specific experiences. These experiences are ones that bring joy, entertainment, fun and laughter, or even very moving profound emotional states. It is important to know the kinds of experiences to seek out because there is no one formula that suits or is relevant to everybody. It is also true that there is a great deal of emphasis within the marketing world telling you what you should invest in. Our media-soaked world bombards us with information: In the inimitable lyrics of Bob Dylan "

"Advertising signs that con you into thinking you're the one that can do what's never been done, than can win what's never been won, meantime life goes on all around you" (written 40 years before the new age bestseller "The Secret"). We are sold ideas about what will bring us fulfilment and happiness. We have to be careful how we respond to these influences. If not, we will become programmed to understand the pursuit of happiness in a way that could easily lead us away from what will truly fulfil us".

French philosopher Jean Baudrillard has brilliantly described how modern Western society has become a slave to media influence. Our very definitions of our selves are now a focus of advertising and marketing. We live in a commodity culture, and define our value by these commodities. The 'use value' of commodities is no longer the primary reasons for why we buy them. A car for example has a use value, namely to get us from A to B. In this situation we would consider buying a car for that purpose. However, the 'sign value' of any particular type of car is what it says about us, and what we feel by owning it. This generalises to all commodities from kitchens to clothes. It is a function of consumer society to keep an unending cycle of commodities available, to change styles and fashions so that a whole raft of commodities becomes obsolete. These then need to be replaced so that new ones can be sold. Accordingly, Baudrillard argues that modern culture has become the production and consumption of signs.

In the absence of a clear sense of identity, the advertising and marketing world will provide one for you. Only last week I was chatting with a friend who told me that her car loan was now fully paid and she was considering changing her car. From other conversations I know that this person is very dissatisfied with her job, and would love to go back to education and follow a career path that involves working with children. It did not to seem to dawn on her that changing her car would compromise her possibilities. It seemed a natural thing to do. This is the effect of constant exposure to being taught how to be in this world by a system whose purpose is to get you to engage in the accumulation of commodities. Jonathan Singer explains *"The middle class in the United States in this century has been able to purchase not only the necessities of life- decent housing an adequate diet, suitable clothing, health care but has been prevailed upon to buy a whole host of non-necessities, even luxuries, made available by capitalist enterprise. (of course, being constantly surrounded by luxuries makes one think of them more as necessities.) By now a family that owns just one automobile confesses to the world that it occupies only a low socioeconomic stratum in our society. Automobiles, recreation vehicles, boats, luxury homes, designer clothes microwave ovens and frozen foods that eliminate the ordeal of cooking, cell phones personal computers and access to the internet a vast assortment of appliances radios, TVs VCRs and many more items have all become household fixtures. Every year or two the previous incarnation of a luxury item is made obsolete by a new, improved (and more expensive) version. Desires that were previously unknown to the human race are brought to white heat by the advertising industry promoting items to be purchased on unlimited credit."*

Buying commodities often has a short-term emotional impact. That new car will lose its shine after a few weeks. And unless it is a spectacular model, you will see lots more of them which ultimately dilute its sign value that tells the world of your success, coolness, achievement, modesty or whatever its meaning is to you. Returning to my friend's dilemma about changing her car: the money for that car could buy many experiences that would enrich her in ways that could last a lifetime. Most of us when we draw near the end of our lives and we search through our treasure chest of memories will not have the day of the new washing machine, flat screen television or luxury handbag high on our list!! If your life carries a 'meaning vacuum', there is an enormous pressure and seduction for you to fill this vacuum with commodities and their symbolisms.

My own society has seen this in action in the past ten years. These years were marked out by enormous economic growth occurring in the aftermath of the collapse of the influence of the Catholic Church. These two events combined to create what was called the "Celtic Tiger". In the context of a spiritual vacuum people borrowed money like there was no tomorrow, they accumulated toys of all sorts, foreign apartments, new cars, helicopters for more than a few, and so on and so forth. The aftermath of the economic crash, saw a significant rise in suicides, especially among those whose identity was bound up in the signs they had bought. It is tragic to think that a man might kill himself rather than face the shame of not being able to get to the Galway races by helicopter. How deep the damage to such a person's humanity.

There is nothing wrong with enjoying commodities in themselves, but I believe that such unhindered accumulation was masking an emptiness and spiritual poverty that began to characterise our society. The consequences are, however, horrendous. The human cost to many hardworking ordinary decent people is profound. Many now find themselves in a level of debt that will soak away their financial resources for at least a decade. This leads to being trapped economically in a way that many married women found themselves throughout the centuries. They were trapped economically by marriage to the man who held all the economic power. Nowadays many people are married to their bank. Unable to access or have income that allows some measure of economic freedom leads to hopelessness and despair. Without your own clear set of meanings that have grown and matured through reflection and self-awareness it is a very simple matter to buy into the 'made-to-measure' model presented by the marketing and advertising industries. Philosopher/Comedian George Carlin said it well when he described people "buying s*** they don't need with money they don't have"

As noted above this has happened on a grand scale here in Ireland during the early 2000's. Politicians courted the population with the promise of unending wealth, the banks sold money to them to fund this illusion, and the property developers built more and more houses and charged way beyond the cost of construction. People bought into the ideology of accumulation and now are suffering the consequences. The lesson from these mistakes is: Avoid buying commodities for their sign value, rather: Buy experiences for their soul value. The problem is that to buy anything you need money, and for a great many who bought into the notion of accumulation of commodities as a path to meaning, they now have very little money to invest in the very things/experiences that have true lasting value.

What then are the experiences you should try to cultivate, or in some situations to buy? An example from my own life may be useful here. Many years ago I went on a package holiday to Egypt that involved a 7 day cruise on the Nile. After a trip to the Valley of the Kings we embarked on our trip. Each day involved visiting historic sites and monuments to that time in history. At the temple of Carnac (I think), the tour guide told the story of the Roman conquest and showed us the scars on the temple columns where the Roman soldiers sharpened their swords. As I traced by finger along one such scar, I was transported back to the historic scene. In my mind's eye I could see the chiselled expression of the Roman centurion, the rope like muscles in his arm, short in stature, as was the case of that time, the armour glinting under the bright African sun, the dust, the smells and whinnying of horses, the grunts of camels all translated as if by magic through my finger along the stone column. I was awoken from my reverie by the voice of one of the party as he said to his wife in a strong cockney accent "it's all the same really innit"! What, for me, was a deeply moving and memorable experience was for him a rather boring trip in a very hot climate where alcohol was hard to get and diarrhoea easy. On the return flight I sat beside a young woman who told me that she didn't leave the hotel for two weeks. I was fascinated that she chose Egypt of all places to spend her holidays. The same sun shines on Torremolinos, the drink is cheaper and the night life much better.

This example tells us that different experiences are meaningful for different people. Perhaps my fellow tourist would have enjoyed the tunnels of Vietnam, the Louvre, the Indianapolis 500 or the world darts championship!! Who knows? The Egypt trip was a very nourishing and spiritually affirming experience for me. On reflection it is easy to see why. From the time I was a little boy I have been deeply curious about life, about the human condition, and about history. My grandmother used to remark to my mother that she was worried about me because I was always reading! I am an intrepidly curious person with a passion for learning. My visit to Egypt therefore touched so many aspects of my own unique self: my interest in history, in heroism and myth, my sense of being part of a world of knowledge that started in that cradle of civilisation. It was a joyful celebration of my own little place in the universe. Others who do not share these core values would not be nourished or affirmed in this way. That is neither right nor wrong, it's just different. Whatever you have a passion for gives you the guidance of the kind of experiences to pursue. The key thing here is to understand that you have limited resources of time, energy and money. So, when you invest in one thing you are not investing in another. If you let the seduction of commodity consumerism enslave you then you will not have the resources to invest in what helps you to embrace, cherish and enrich your own unique life.

Who you want to engage with

Thus far we have looked at religious belief and practice, sport, parenthood, work, money and creative action as sources of meaning. Each of these can be tailored to an individual life. We can give up or change our religious devotions, stop attending a course on astronomy because we discovered that it was not really right for us, go back to college and study something that holds our interest. We can take up hang gliding, fishing or art. However, if you discover becoming a parent was in fact not a good idea for your life, you cannot simply abandon the responsibility, because it involves the welfare of others for whom you are responsible. There are some decisions and choices that have long term consequences that are neither easily nor morally dispensable. This takes us into the arena of human relationships.

All relationships involve a transfer of emotional energy. And emotional energy is a major resource that you cannot afford to waste. Many relationships are simply a matter of habit; they occurred often accidentally and now make up the social aspect of our lives. How many of us truly evaluate if our friendships, companions are good for us? And what does it mean that a relationship is good for us. Scott Peck, in his classic work "The Road Less Travelled" gives a simple but very effective measuring tool. Simply put, a good relationship is one in which both people grow spiritually by virtue of being in that relationship! A key word here is 'both'. Our relationships need to be reciprocal. The transfer of energy needs to go both ways. A relationship in which one person exhausts their resources for the sake of another who gives little back is a dysfunctional relationship. The one exception here is that of charity or care where you have decided that part of your life task is to take care of someone. This is a work/creative relationship. The area of relationships is so vast that I will dedicate the chapter following to it.

Resources for Change.

The discussion so far has outlined the direction toward which to direct yourself in terms of a more fulfilling and authentic life. Direction alone is however only part of the story. The other part is the investment of resources. In general, our resources can be categorised into five general areas: Money, time, energy, knowledge and support.

Money

Our financial resources seem to be an obvious place to start when we want to look at how to go about making changes to or taking on new directions in life. The way we spend our money tells us something about our priorities and values. For those who have very little money the challenges of affording the luxury of making choices is of course very significant. But even small amounts of money can be used to help broaden one's experiences and possibilities in life. A simple example here is that of someone with modest financial resources who spends a substantial amount of it on cigarettes. Addiction to nicotine or alcohol seriously compromises a person's financial resources and prevents the use of money for better healthier and more life enhancing activities. I do not have any strong value judgement against a person's choice to smoke or drink, rather I am saying that the cost of these activities can soak up resources that could be better used, if that person has a vision for themselves that requires money, as almost everything in life does.

It is useful to recall the earlier discussion about living in a capitalist consumer economy. The lifeblood of the economy is based on consumption. That means that, from the time of our birth, to the style of casket in which we are buried, we are treated by market forces as units of consumption. We are targets in a myriad of ways to spend our money on everything from disposable razors with 5 blades with lubricating strip! Skinny lattes with vanilla shots, handbags costing five thousand euro, regular phone upgrades and so on and do forth. On and on, the interminable deluge of marketing information calls on us to spend, spend, spend. There is no arena in a modern society that is not driven by the economic reality of consumption. There are no hallowed grounds or sacred areas not affected. Education, for example, often considered one of those pure areas of human endeavour is, in fact, massively influenced by finance. Ivan Illich's 'Deschooling Society' tells the story of how educational institutions must sell their courses in order to keep afloat. Certification ensures that more and more education is required as one type of qualification is replaced by another.

I had a personal encounter with this problem recently. A close relative wanted to apply for training in clinical psychology, an area that when I was a student one could apply for with a good honour's degree. She discovered that of ten applicants accepted for training in one university, all had Ph.Ds already. They had already gone through undergraduate and two post graduate degree courses lasting up to 7 years in order to be accepted into a training course for clinical psychology. Students are now the customers of fee-paying University which can lead to a serious conflict on interest in terms of educational standards. It is a difficult business decision to fail students who are paying thousands of dollars for their place in the institution. Learning is promoted and new markets for the sale of education are identified. Medicine and health are other good examples with concerns that new diseases are being identified, not on the basis of scientific research but on the need to sell pharmaceuticals. When we understand the degree to which we are exposed to a constant effort to get hold of our financial resources we can become a bit more cautions and learn to ask the question, how does my spending this money help me toward my life goals?

Time.

It can be said that of all our resources, time is the one we can never replace. When I was a young post graduate student, I came across a useful exercise in Irvin Yalom's book 'Existential Psychotherapy.'

This involves drawing a line across a page and putting the letter B at the beginning and D at the end. B refers to my birth and D my death. Then place the letter X on the place where I am on this life line. And although few of us can predict the time of our demise we can follow the general statistical norm for the sake of the exercise. The X refers to where I am on the line. I can remember where the X was on the line between B and D when I was 23 yr. old and where it is now: on the final quarter!

This exercise can have a rather sobering effect. It can keep us focused on the responsibility to take account of our mortality as well as reminding us that time is not a renewable resource. As in the inimitable words of Red the character played by Morgan Freeman in Shawshank Redemption "We either get busy living or get busy dying.

Energy

Our energy can be understood as physical, mental and emotional. We really only fully appreciate the resource of energy when it becomes depleted through illness. The old adage that 'your health is your wealth' usually bypasses us until we are laid low. So much of our construction of life is dependent on energy. It is often the case that we spend it without really reflecting on whether this or that activity is worth the cost. One of the most expensive demands on emotional energy lies in the way we construct our relationships with others. Some relationships are massively draining. Certain professions whereby the care of others is involved recognise that caring relationships can lead to emotional exhaustion and burnout. In these situations, there is education and training available for professional carers so that they do not damage themselves as a result of losing the balance between the care of others and the care of the self. What is not so clear is the nature of personal relationships that can also be exhausting, and certain relationship patterns, best known as co-dependency can become a life-threatening disorder. I will examine this in more detail in the chapter following.

Physical and mental energy is expended during other types of work. Ironically, boredom can deplete energy, leaving people fatigued and drained. Once again it is our responsibility to examine how much energy we spend in any given aspect of our lives and to consider if there is enough left over for those areas that are important to our needs for fulfilment and joy. A perfect example is the exhausted couple who climb into bed every night and are too tired to make love. They are, either individually or collectively, starving their relationship of one of the key elements in a happy partnership.

Summary

This chapter explored the issue of our life tasks and the meaning and purpose we choose for our lives. It showed how we can use the faculties of memory and imagination as part of reflective living so that we can design our life project. It also showed that this project involves what we believe in terms of religious meaning, the things we create that say something of importance to us, the relationships we engage in, and the experiences we cultivate. The topic of relationships is examined in more detail in the next chapter.

Chapter 5.
Authentic Relationships.

And did you get what
you wanted from this life, even so?
I did.
And what did you want?
To call myself beloved, to feel myself beloved on the earth.
Late Fragment: Raymond Carver

Introduction

The focus thus far has been primarily on what we can control, and how we can widen the range of events over which we can exert power. There are, of course, certain aspects of life over which we can exert very little control. Nowhere in our lives, however, is this truer than in our relationships. It is a truism that we cannot change other people. And it is in this arena that the greatest difficulties arise. Once you invite people into your life you give them access to your heart, to your energy and to your resources. It is precisely because of this that we need to understand very clearly what it will cost us to have certain people in our lives, and equally what benefits to our being in the world that will come about because we have given them that place.

The work I do often unfortunately makes me a witness to the carnage and suffering that accrue in the lives of individuals because of the choices they make for the sake of relationships. This, I am aware, may give me a somewhat skewed or biased view and I hope that I do not communicate that relationships are always fraught with problems or difficulties. They also can bring with them joy, healing, encouragement and consolation. It is these latter aspects that are so important and essential to our lives. And it is imperative that we learn how to 'people' our lives with those who bring these gifts to us, and that we become individuals who offer these in return. The rest of this chapter is a discussion on how to improve existing relationships and choosing ones that are better for us.

Why do people stay in bad relationships?

Anyone who has had a close friend, colleague or family member who stayed for years being diminished and hurt in a relationship will have had the experience of deep frustration and confusion as to why such things happen. They will have chatted with their own spouse/partner or friends asking the question how can such a lovely/intelligent/capable and competent person keep doing this to themselves. It is a conundrum that is difficult to understand because on the surface it makes no sense. Throughout my years in the field of counselling I have seen again and again the process of peoples' lives being enormously damaged by staying in what I call toxic relationships. There are however a few reasons for this rather common occurrence. Although every relationship is unique there is generally a mix of two or three overlapping dynamics that cause people to remain in long term chronic anguish or low-level despair and hurt. The more common elements are: fear, ignorance, low self-worth, children, money, intrepid but misplaced optimism, guilt and immature moral development.

Fear

There are many things in life that people fear. Some are appropriate, fear of loss, of dangerous dogs, of drunk drivers and so on and so forth. It is normal and healthy to fear these things. And sometimes it is important to face one's fears...but not always. 'Feel the fear and do it anyway' is sometimes valid, and sometimes very stupid. There are people in their graves because the applied this maxim in the wrong place. Fear then is part of living; it is to a large extent, a useful and protective emotion.

In bad relationships, fear usually keeps the individual hanging in there for two reasons, fear of abandonment and loneliness, and in more violent relationships fear for one's physical safety. Fear of loneliness can be a crippling concern. It is not surprising that solitary confinement is used as a form of punishment and torture. We are social creatures designed to make close attachments that bring a sense of belonging and connection. The most intense form is that of lifelong companionship with our mate. Some people stay together unhappily because they believe that the loneliness of being single would be worse. Fear for one's safety is also worthy of mention. Those who are victimised and bullied in a relationship often stay because they believe that if they try to leave they will be in danger. There are plenty of examples to show that this is a reality for some. It is a very difficult challenge to decide to leave in such a situation and it is crucial to access all the legal and social/emotional support available in such an event.

Ignorance

I use the word ignorance here, not in a critical sense but in the original sense of the word. I mean it here in the sense whereby I can say that I am ignorant when it comes to astrophysics, geology, and soap operas. In other words, I just don't know much about these subjects. Some people stay in unhappy relationships because they don't know any better. These are often people who grew up in unhappy families and therefore have little expectations for happiness with their mate. Often, they do not reflect much on what a fulfilling relationship might be. In essence they are living out the type of relationships that prevailed through most of our history. As discussed earlier, marriage was not for happiness and fulfilment, it was for creating a family and providing for one's children. Happiness was an extra and rare enough.

Low Self Worth

One of the most common and popularised ideas in modern psychology is that of self-worth. It has been examined in some detail in the earlier part of this book. Self-worth is a notion that was to a large extent unheard of a century ago. Its discovery has had an enormous influence in understanding why people do the things they do. Low self-worth is a condition whereby an individual places little or no value on themselves. Those who suffer this condition will generally react to it in one of two ways. One, by over reacting and trying too hard to get attention and value from the outside world by showing off, seeking attention by over-achieving, raging with jealousy against other who have more the he/she has, unable to give to others or to accept any criticism. On the other hand the low self-worth person tends to devalue any of their accomplishments, have a high tolerance for being mistreated by others, low expectations for being treated well and respected, and in general they accept a diminished life. And woe betides those who marry each other if they come from the two poles of this disorder.

Children

Perhaps the most poignant reasons for people staying unhappily together is that of their concern for their children. Of all the reasons discussed here, this is one that, in certain situations, is an authentic reason for staying. More specifically, I am of the view that bringing children into this world is perhaps the most responsible act made by a human being. To my mind the responsibility to ones' children, supersedes that of commitment to personal happiness. This view is somewhat controversial and I should be somewhat nuanced in expressing it. There is much truth in the notion that children will fare better if they are given proper care from both parents if these parents are separated from each other. This is the ideal solution to a situation where the parents have reached the end of their relationship/partnership. Children do not flourish in an environment where there is great conflict and/or unhappiness between their parents. However, there are situations where this is not possible. Thus, in certain situations where children will suffer too much (separation almost always causes some hurt to children), the decision to leave should be postponed. The specific situation I refer to here arises when a person will lose proper involvement with his/her children, and will be leaving them in the care of someone who is a negative or even destructive force. Classic example being leaving children in the care of an alcoholic or otherwise mentally disturbed parent. Legal custody solutions here are often flawed as the toxic effect of a parent can quite easily be disguised.

Money

There is an old saying that 'love goes out the window when poverty comes in the door'. It is not surprising that relationships can collapse when adversity strikes, and financial difficulties are a particular type of adversity. It is however a different case when someone chooses to stay in an unhappy relationship because it gives them access to the financial resources of another. It is very rarely about the money itself but rather the resources that such money can buy, including the psychological aspects such as the sign value of commodities discussed in an earlier chapter. It is a form of selling oneself to another. The person sells out their relationship needs for the social status, clothes, commodities, membership of a social set and such like that they would otherwise not be able to enjoy. It is a life choice and for those who make that choice it is clear that they believe that the benefits outweigh the cost of personal relationship unhappiness. In the end it is rarely worth it. The cost to one's personal growth and fulfilment is rarely worth the few material gains.

Family

One of the most important places for learning how to build relationships occurs in immediate family. Our first introduction to being with others, communicating, and getting our needs met happens in the early years of life inside the home. These relationships to a large degree set up a template for how we relate to others throughout our lives. It is therefore a considerable task to examine the nature of these relationships, especially when we realise that perhaps our way of connecting with others is not working.

Two of the most crucial ingredients in healthy relationships are respect, and empathy. These two provide pillars on which healthy relationships of all kinds are built in our adulthood. In families where each member is treated with respect the people grow to acknowledge the differences that make each person unique. Respect also prevents the misuse or abuse of others in the family. The outcome then is that the members of that kind of family grow to respect the differences in others as well as developing a strong moral standing in relation to choosing not to abuse or misuse others. In families where such respect is not a feature, the outcome is that some become perpetrators of disrespect, simply using others for their own ends. Others become victims and therefore tend to develop a high tolerance for being badly treated by others.

Empathy is the other pillar of a healthy relationship. It is the quality that allows a person to have some emotional identification with the feelings of another. It is not limited to human beings because it has been observed in the animal kingdom. Elephants, chimpanzees and dolphins are particularly notable for their expressions of empathy for members of their group who suffer. In humans however, empathy is the absolute essential quality that gives one human being the ability to care and love another. All the studies of the great evils of the world show that in order for people to become cruel towards another they have to switch off their empathy for that person. Military systems are designed to train their personnel in such a way that they have no empathy for the enemy. They do this by consistently dehumanising them. Thus, in the course of the Vietnam war, the Vietnamese were called slopes, slants, gooks and the like by American soldiers. In Nazi Germany Jewish people were depicted in propaganda as lice and rats. Once the programming of dehumanisation is complete the soldier or civilian no longer feels towards the enemy the feelings that he has for his own kind. In the absence of empathy there is a wide-open space for destruction and cruelty. When empathy returns it leads to remorse. Empathy is then a crucial element in advanced and evolved relationships. When you invite someone into your life in a very personal way it is important to evaluate just how much empathy they have towards you. If you find yourself consistently trying to explain yourself then it is likely that it is a dysfunctional relationship, and one to avoid.

Friendship

My mother used to say "Michael if you count your friends in life on the fingers of one hand you are very blessed indeed". There was great wisdom in this because true friendship is a very special and sacred thing. Many people live out their whole lives without true friends. Sure, they may have many acquaintances, work colleagues, golf buddies, coffee morning pals but no one who they can truly share their intimate self with. Someone who will listen with care and concern, will have the courage to confront when needed and someone who will arrive in the dark times that mark out everybody's life at some stage or other, someone with whom you feel affirmed and respected. And someone whose company you enjoy.

I remember a remark made once to me by a woman with whom I was close. We were talking about love and being in love. She had worked hard at understanding herself and getting over many obstacles in her life regarding relationships. She said in passing " Michael, I don't tell people any more that I love them, I tell them that I love myself when I am in their company". This remark had a big impact as I reflected on the notion that maybe this is the benchmark of all good relationships. When we reflect on our relationships, friendships, acquaintances and lovers, maybe our inquiry needs to be less about how we feel about the other, but more about how do we feel about ourselves when we have been with this person.

I spend a lot of time with people who have been damaged at the hands of others. I continue to be amazed at the capacity that some people have to tolerate suffering inflicted by people who pretend, or even believe that they love the person they are hurting. There is something very wrong in the developed world in this regard. There is something very wrong in the way people are educated about relationships. I cannot do full justice to this topic here because it would require a book of its own. All I can attempt here is to suggest that an enlightened and examined life requires an understanding that we cannot give others the right to hurt us, and that if they do so we need to develop the strength and courage to leave such people behind. I am not talking here of the small incidental hurts that can occur in any relationship, I am talking about the type of relationships that lead people to become damaged in virtue of being in that relationship.

One of the more interesting dynamics I have discovered over the years as I have reflected on the problem of destructive relationships is the dynamic between power and attachment. For some people the strongest element of their relationship to others is that of power. They need to feel in control of the relationship and that sense of control makes them feel good. They are not particularly interested in intimacy or emotional attachment. Their capacity for love, care and support tends to be practical and concrete. For others their primary need in the relationship is attachment and a sense of belonging. In this case the loving bond is strongly emotional and spiritual. If we make a crude division of people into these categories we can understand at least one source of major difficulty in relationships. Add to this a very common error in how people operate in relationships. This is what is called attribution error. Attribution error is a psychological phenomenon whereby people mistakenly attribute certain qualities to others and base their communication with that person on the basis of these mistaken projections. The most common attribution error is the one whereby we assume that others are like ourselves. So, when an attachment-oriented person meets a power-oriented person the potential for disaster looms. The one who seeks attachment believes that the other seeks the same, and goes about explaining how this can succeed. The one who seeks power simply uses the information to keep control.

In and of itself this difference in orientation does not always lead to disaster. However, it is a very useful example when it comes to understanding what we seek in relationship and the kind of relationships that are right for us. Awareness of attribution error and projections are an important part of evaluating what is going on in our relationships. The examined life requires examining our relationships. It means standing back and taking time to reflect on what it is that makes that relationship worth holding on to. Has it outlived its part in your life? Relationships are living things. Like ourselves, they are either growing, stagnating or dying. Some have the potential to outlast the lives of those in them. This means that if we lived three lifetimes the friendship would still sustain. Others have died and are only being maintained by the life support machine of a sense of duty and politeness.

Building good friendship takes commitment and care. It requires knowing the kind of person that "fits" with your unique self, and good friendship is also an essential ingredient in a long-lasting love relationship. This brings us again to the difference between the constructed self and the true self. If we don't have a clear notion of the distinction then we can fill our lives with people who relate to our constructed self, as we in turn relate to theirs.

I remember well a conversation on this topic with a client who spoke of feeling alienated and upset because she felt like an outsider. She made valiant efforts to impress people, to partake in their lives and yet they all seemed in some way or other to reject or at least not to include her. As we discussed this difficulty, she described what she was looking for in her friendships and it became clear that she was trying to insert herself into a group of people with whom she had no natural affinity. Deeper analysis showed that she was operating out of the construction of social acceptability. The seductive attraction of the - upper middle-class commodity accumulation-based image- drew her in. Her feelings of shame from early life left her vulnerable to believe that without the accoutrements of 'success' she was a failure. This individual was, at a core level, a bit of a hippy, a non-conformist with interest in art and anarchy, who despite her valiant effort could not jettison these in order to dress both physically and psychologically as a nice, conforming middle-class mom. Therein lay the problem. She resolved this difficulty by leaving behind these efforts, going to art college, and meeting people more like her true self, people who were a better fit. In time she lost that feeling of alienation and aloneness, made new and more enjoyable acquaintances and had a different pool of people from which to choose who could become friends. You cannot manufacture friends. There must be a natural fit, and unless you understand who you truly are, you will often find yourself groping in the dark when it comes to choosing the people who accompany you through life.

With regard to friendship then there are two considerations. First, does the person fit with my true self. Do they share enough common ground with my core values in life to be able to have harmony? Have we enough common interests to be able to enjoy the spark of connection? The second relates to the impact their company has on me. How do I feel when I spend time with this person? Do I feel supported, encouraged, challenged, and respected? Just as in the earlier chapters the focus here is on how the choices we make lead us to inhibit or compromise our lives on one hand, or to enhance and help us to flourish on the other. Am I enthusiastic, uplifted, relieved, affirmed, or am I bored, insecure, let down or defeated? This inquiry is crucial because 'time' is the one aspect of life we cannot replace. Spending time with people who damage us or who cause us to lose faith in ourselves and our life project is time wasted. And again, the sculpting tool of freedom is the one you use to let go, to move away from such people and to move toward those who affirm you.

In the earlier chapter I spoke of trauma being a life experience that can prevent people from being able to make choices. This can be particularly relevant where relationships are concerned. A person can do the analysis above and conclude that a relationship is bad for them but find it emotionally impossible to leave it. In such a situation that person still has the choice to get help to support them and to give them the guidance they need. A degree of freedom still exists even in the most entrapped circumstances. Staying in damaging relationships is a choice and ultimately that choice can destroy a person's life. The main function of counselling/therapy is to help people gain the strength to live better and more fulfilling lives. This sometimes means helping them recover from psychic wounds inflicted during childhood, wounds that may still be affecting their happiness and ability to manage life. Counselling can also involve helping people understand more clearly their motivations. It can focus on developing better communication skills, or then again simply help the individual to clarify where they want to go and design a better map for getting there. All these are the remit of good counselling/therapy. When you feel stuck in life, effective counselling is the profession developed to help you become unstuck.

Recently, I met with a lady in just such a situation. Married to an active alcoholic, she was frantically trying to find some way to fix him, to get him to see sense and to get help for his problem. As we spoke, I could see that her attention was almost completely focused on her husband, and his chaotic, and self-destructive behaviour. Each time I tried to get her to look at herself and the effect his behaviour was having on her life, she seemed to drift away with a look of confusion. I gave her the bad news that she had to decide whether or not to save herself. I explained that once you have given the power of your own happiness, safety, security into someone else's hands they then have control of your life. If they disintegrate, they will take you down with them. Her only hope was to take back power over her own life before she too would be destroyed. As she left the session I reflected on our conversation and concluded that I would, most likely, not see her again for some time. She will probably go looking for a different kind of help that will involve her learning techniques to control or fix her husband.

These will fail, and hopefully in time she will return to me, or someone like me who can help her embark on the journey of retrieving her independence and inner strength. Paradoxically, this has a far better chance of having the effect of saving her marriage, although that is not the goal.

Romantic Love

Discussing friendship is a far easier task than that of sexual and romantic relationships. This is because the complexities of attachment bonds that are sexual/romantic are truly enormous. The following is a somewhat sketchy analysis of some of the pitfalls as well as some of the peaks that romantic sexual love brings to a person's life.

I use the word romantic here advisedly as a way of describing the relationship that has the character of being-in-love. This is what psychologists call 'pair bonding', a description that, in my opinion, fits better with an advertisement for adhesive that a human relationship!! Anyway, language aside, we are now discussing relationships that generally start by falling in love, sexual attraction, having sex and the decision to commit to a marriage or partnership.

Because this book is about authenticity, fulfilment, and meaning we must first examine what how these relate to sexual and romantic relationships. And in doing so I find it useful to dispel some illusions that are in the way.

Falling in Love.

Perhaps one of the most characteristic feature of modern Western society is that glamorisation of the state of romantic love. Everywhere we look and listen we see and hear its virtues being extolled, all in the context of massive failure of marriage as an arrangement by which people commit and remain with each other. Romantic love is a new idol. Ernest Becker writes wonderfully when he says *"The love partner becomes the divine ideal within which to fulfil one's life. All spiritual and moral needs now become focused in one individual. Spirituality, which once referred to another dimension of being, is now brought down to this earth and gives form in another individual human being. Salvation itself is no longer referred to an abstraction like God, but can be sought in the beatification of the other".* And, of course, no human being can bear this burden or live up to this expectation. This, in turn, means that falling in love is never a sufficient basis for an authentic lasting relationship. What then is it all about, and where does falling in love fit in making a sexual attraction into an authentic and abiding bond?

Perhaps one of the most powerful experiences in life is that of falling in love with someone. It is a great phrase because it captures the sense of being out of control. To fall is to lose your ground, to be at the mercy of gravity, to grapple wildly to hang on to something, to save yourself. Falling in love is a delicious and powerful experience. But it is just that, an experience. It is worth exploring it in some detail because it leads people to make choices while under the influence of its power that can have lasting consequences for their lives.

Falling is love is, to a large degree, an altered state of consciousness not unlike those produced by mind altering substances, except that the body and brain don't require any outside chemical assistance (most drug experiences work by getting the brain to over produce certain neurotransmitters and thereby create the psychological/emotional effect). When you fall in love the brain produces its own chemical overload. The effects are so powerful that most people want to keep it forever. A good comparison is that of the heroin addict. For most addicts the first hit is so profound that they can spend the rest of their lives slowly destroying themselves trying to recapture the experience. Drug induced states often cause the user to experience illusions and delusions, some are positive some are negative. Some examples are: Ecstasy: 'I love everyone', Heroin: 'I am one with the universe', Cocaine: 'I can do anything', Cannabis: 'everyone is watching' me, LSD: 'I am the Devil'. Certain illusions are also common during the experience of falling in love These are produced by the powerful overload of neurotransmitters evoked by the presence of the love 'object'.

This powerful and special experience is not just sexual attraction. You can experience sexual attraction to a prostitute, a television model, or any stranger walking down the street. *Only Fans* is probably the most iconic representation of the commodification of sexual attraction currently available. Falling in love is more complex. It is a heady mix of sexual attraction, projection, infantile dependency, old wounds in need of healing, idealisation of the other and much more. It is a naturally occurring, often very positively delightful and life enhancing experience.

It has, however, very little to do with a relationship. Falling in love is an extremely powerful transient psychosexual connection between people. A good relationship is an attachment based on shared goals, friendship, sexual attraction, lovemaking, trust and respect. The essential element here, in terms of living authentically, is for one to merge into the other. Our recent culture has supported, and proclaimed the myth that one leads naturally to the other. As a result, there is untold suffering as people contract themselves to each other based on the altered state that often has already dissolved but the couple believe that they can still find it. One of the most destructive types of relationship occurs when two individuals who are unsuited to each other, fall in love for a period, and then engage in a chronic and sometimes lifelong effort to change the other. In general, this takes the form of one person trying everything in their power to get the other person to love and respect them. In this situation it is often the case that the one who is trying so hard to get their partner's loves and respect has very low self-esteem and often comes from a childhood marked out by emotional deprivation of some kind. They have carried into their adulthood the scars of feeling unworthy and unloved. In turn, they choose a person who in truth does not love them, or perhaps is so damaged that their ability to love and respect another is profoundly damaged. The capacity to fall in love is no predictor of the ability to sustain a loving and respectful relationship. Let us look at some of the illusions that occur in the altered state of consciousness called "being in love."

The Illusion of Necessity.

In my seminars I make the quip that if anyone tells you "I cannot live without you": give them my card. The illusion of necessity is the overwhelming feeling that this person is essential to your being able to live a fulfilled life. It is closely related to the notion that this is 'The One'. Modern literature abounds with this illusion. I remember being at a seminar on marriage in my early twenties, organised by the local church where the speaker said, "don't marry a woman/man you can live with. Marry someone you cannot live without"! Here's my response 30 years later. If you meet someone you cannot live without, end the relationship because you are not mature enough for one, and go for help! Or maybe less drastically, just get help.

This aspect of the being in love is often a psychological regression. The only person is the world that you could not live without is your mother or mother substitute. This is a factual reality. In infancy you are absolutely helpless and utterly dependent on the care of a mother or mother substitute. You will die without her. The experience of falling in love often triggers the long-buried traces of that dependency and because we are creatures of meaning we have to make sense of it. So, we get to believe that we cannot survive without this person because that is what it "feels" like. Paradoxically, those who have been abandoned early in life or who have significant trauma in those early dependency relationships are most likely to suffer horrendous pain at the risk of losing the one they "love". So much so that some of these unfortunates have "loved" their partner so intensely that they had to beat them up or even kill them when they tried to leave! I recently viewed the Netflix series I am a Stalker. It provides a very useful insight into the psychology of people who turn the Illusion of Necessity into a guide for terribly destructive behaviour, ruining their own lives and the lives of their victims.

The Illusion of Completion

From Greek mythology and also the Genesis creation myth comes the notion that male and female are incomplete halves of some idealistic whole. In the Judeo-Christian scheme, the whole is the man (Eve being produced from the rib of Adam). If someone tells you that you complete them, I suggest a gentle invitation to them that perhaps they should complete themselves. This may appear somewhat cynical but it is to my mind an essential point. I am not saying here that a relationship will not bring great possibilities for joy, companionship, mutual understanding, helping each other out. I am saying that no other person can complete your own identity. This is an illusion based on the presence of large doses of serotonin, dopamine and Oxytocin in certain tracts of your brain. Not unlike the sense of fusion or oneness created by long meditative practices or a strong dose of opium.

There is another element of the need for completion that has grown more prevalent in recent times. We saw in an earlier chapter that many people try to hide in the herd in order to avoid the fear that comes with individuality and the consequent threat of rejection. This reminds us that, as human beings, we are troubled by a fear of insignificance and meaninglessness on one hand, and a desire to be part of something great and eternal, on the other. For most of our history our religious symbols and rituals have resolved this dilemma by giving us a program of meanings, including a promise of some kind of eternal existence. In recent decades all of this in Western culture has faded away under the growth of rationalism, and consumerism. The centre no longer holds in our religious traditions. As a result, there is a need to find a new way to sooth the raw edges of our temporal and insignificant lives. The growth of faith in romantic love does just that. We now place responsibility for our sense of the eternal and mystical completion in the hands of our lovers. And that is far too much responsibility, and will inevitably fail.

The Illusion of Eternal Happiness

I remember well that joyous moment of being in love (of which I have had a few) when I said to myself, "I could live in the corner of an attic with this woman, I love her so much". The relationship ended six weeks later. And that without even trying the living in an attic option! It is well known that when we are in a very heightened emotional state our rational capabilities are reduced. This is a key part of our survival. If my child runs out in front of a bus, I don't have time to rationalise the situation. That part of my mind switches off to allow instinct and adrenaline to take over as I launch out in disregard for my own safety to pull my child out of danger. The heightened emotional state of being 'in love' causes us to lose our rational footing. We become unable to examine in any reasoned way if the person is really suitable, and what it will take to build a lasting relationship with him or her. Rather we indulge the illusion that we will be forever happy in this bubble of 'love'. A client of mine recently brought this home to me. I asked her how her relatively new relationship was going. She quipped "oh it's great, I'm still in the eejit stage". Such a good insight to be able to enjoy the intensity of the phase of the relationship while remaining aware that her critical faculties were not fully operating. Nietzsche would have been proud of her. He similarly comments "A pair of powerful spectacles has sometimes sufficed to cure a person in love".

The Illusion of Recognition

This illusion is best understood in the phrase that often occurs between in-love couples: "I feel like I know you all my life". Or for the more reincarnation oriented; "I feel we must have known each other in a past life". There is some truth in this experience. It occurs because the 'in love' couple are indeed meeting someone they know very well: Themselves. A trick of the mind called projection was first described in some detail by Freud, and more thoroughly by his daughter Anna. When we meet 'the one' we fall in love with, we project onto that person many of our own psychological characteristics and then fall in love with that mirror image. Sometimes we project aspects of ourselves that we have disconnected from or disowned. Thus, if you have disowned your creativity and bent yourself into the shape of a very practical common sense and logical type, you will find the bohemian and often spirited nonconformist aspects of the creative individual very attractive. Equally, they may have rejected the conforming, common-sense aspects of themselves and will be drawn to the logical structured personality. This is, of course, the basis for the notion that opposites attract. And while this may be true, it is also true that, in general, opposites do not make for good relationships. A useful rule of thumb here is that the more of our own true self that we have disowned the more we will be inclined to over value and overestimate those characteristics in the beloved partner. It is then a logical step to understand that the more self-aware we are the less likely we are to sell out to this illusion.

In modern culture 'being in love' is the first stage of selecting someone to become a life partner. It is the time when intense emotional interchange occurs. The more wounded or fractured we are, the more intense this will be, and the more appalling will be the pain when it falls apart or when the experience begins to wear off. For many couples the next stage is the stage of disillusionment. Michael Gurian explains this very well in "Love's Journey". This stage of disillusionment can last for years, particularly if the couple marry and have family together. The relationship becomes a constant struggle to "get back to what we had". As the true personalities of the couple emerge over time, the projections no longer work, the inner wound of the child in each doesn't heal and rails against the change in the other individual. Of course, the other person has not changed. They are simply becoming more present to the relationship as the couple attempt to carry on with the tasks of living now that the 'drug' of 'being in love' has worn off. This provides the sense to the old proverb 'marry in haste and regret at your leisure'. It is a great problem of modern culture that this early infant stage of relationship is constantly championed as true love. Love songs, movies, romantic novels all support and encourage the myth. As a result, the whole area of love is infantilised.

I have been a witness to the tragic endings of relationships that were simply made from the components of this infantile stage. John is in his fifties. He has fallen in love with someone who he believes is his soul mate. When she decided to leave him, all his unmet childhood dependency needs surfaced and overwhelmed him with grief of abandonment and rejection. He stalks his girlfriend, drinks every night to kill the pain, rails in rage and grief about her, in his mind and heart she is the most wonderful thing that ever happened to him!

As we explore how he can cope better we travel back to his childhood. His childhood was marked out by the endemic cruelty to children carried out in the name of discipline at home and in school. A child of an alcoholic mother who abandoned him to an orphanage he tells the story of the little boy crying himself to sleep at night thinking about his mummy who he believes still wants him. He recounts his various efforts to escape to go back to a mother only to discover again and again that she didn't want him. He survives into adulthood and buries the pain and gets on with his life. He marries a steady but emotionally distant woman. In doing so he found someone who would not threaten his very scarred emotional heart, and is repeating the emotional abandonment of his childhood. They settle down to a dull but effective family arrangement. Then he 'falls in love' with a spirited sexy younger colleague.

All the illusions are there: recognition, completion, eternal bliss, and necessity. The relationship ends and he falls apart. Thankfully he had the sense to get help and to find ways to understand that the person he is 'in love' with doesn't exist except in his fantasy and projection. In time he works out the pain of his past and matures into someone who can have a better relationship. It was, in fact, the best thing that had ever happened to him, but not in the way he thought. He leaves his marriage because it was in fact a holding pattern. It is what I call a Hansel and Gretel relationship based on mutual fear, and the need for security.

John's story tells us much about the effect of fear of abandonment and isolation has on the way we manage being in a relationship. An alternative to the intense dependency often characteristic of such relationship is its opposite: an inability to form satisfying emotional attachment and an avoidance of true intimacy. People who have been hurt in their formative years can resolve to never trust again and thereby engage in steady but unsatisfying relationships on one hand, or a series of sexual conquests or casual flings on the other. Some manage to do both at the same time, a steady business-like arrangement with a spouse and a series of sexual infidelities as well.

If being in love is not an authentic relationship then what is? In general, there are three components that the field of psychology has unearthed in the thinking and research on this topic. These are: desire, friendship and fidelity. Some people are very fortunate in that they fall in love with someone who can become a partner that reflects these qualities. Desire is fairly simple. It is about sexual attraction and a level of sexual compatibility. If the sexual relationship doesn't work reasonably well then the relationship is troubled. Certainly, if sexual problems exist then some help can be brought to bear, but this cannot replace sexual attraction. You either have that or you don't.

Friendship is based on reasonable level of compatibility. I have discussed this topic earlier but people often lose sight of its importance when such emphasis is placed on the sexual and emotional intensities in modern culture. Good relationships that enhance both people are found to a large degree between people who are quite alike in their values, world view, intellect and social skills.

Fidelity is about trust and monogamy. Free love and open relationships were once considered cool. For the most part they don't work. A very good example of a lifelong love relationship is that between Jean Paul Sartre and Simone de Beauvoir. Two towering intellectuals remained together until Sartre died. He was often unfaithful and that was an arrangement that was agreed between them, but not without a cost. De Beauvoir was hurt by his infidelity. And a question always remains, is it acceptable to hurt the one you love in this way.

Marriage

One type of relationship that has predominated human history is that of marriage. It is misleading, however, to discuss marriage as a relationship. Marriage itself is not a relationship; it is a type of contractual arrangement about a relationship. Thus, a marriage can involve a whole range of couple relationships, great ones, horrible ones, happy ones, sad ones and so and so forth.

Marriage is both a legal and moral contract between two people who are in a sexual relationship. Some marriages are those of conveniences such as those entered into for the reasons of attaining visas and the like. This is recognised, however, as a dishonest use of the marital idea.

Rituals that mark the significant passages or transitions in life are a core part of human society. Birth, inclusion in the tribe, the ending of childhood, the introduction to adulthood, marriage, becoming a parent, and dying are the significant transitions and all have some tribal/societal ritual or practice, examples being circumcision, baptism, communion, running the gauntlet. Every society has some form of ritualising the adult bonded sexual relationship. These rituals set the relationship apart as being special and, in some manner, exclusive to the couple in it. Marriage ceremonies are a way of ritualising the choosing of a mate. That is its human cultural meaning.

The importance of social and community pressure to hold the marriage bond in high esteem is based on the reality that the survival of children was dependent on the commitment of the father and mother. The father was the provider and the mother was the nurturer. This is the core template for marriage throughout most communities in human history. A sexual relationship produced children, who were the future of the tribe, and needed to be cared for. The resources for survival depended in large part on the physical prowess and strength of the male. Marriage then became the bedrock of social survival. That all changed in the western world especially with the advent of the industrial revolution, which replaced agrarian society with industrial society. In addition, two crucial changes occurred in the 20th century that has completely undermined the original template for marriage. The first is that widespread use of contraceptives meant that couples could have sex with each other without producing children. This meant that having sex became separate from marriage on a wide scale. There was always sex outside marriage but at great risk of pregnancy and almost always followed by forced marriage because of pregnancy.

A second sea change was that of the women's rights movement which led to women becoming economically independent from men. Women now no longer need men to provide for their children (they can of course choose to if they wish). Women could now choose or plan when to have children, could have a sexual relationship with a man without having to marry him, and vice versa, and did not need to marry to be financially secure. In this context the basis then to marry was for love. This however has caused enormous problems. Marriage is a legally binding contract whose roots lie in its need to coerce people to live together long enough to ensure the care of the children. When the basis for being married changed to the issue of loving fulfilment with each other, all kinds of problems have emerged. This is simply because it is not possible to legislate for happiness in a relationship. It is a contradiction in terms.

As an institution then the marriage contract is a vestigial organ in the evolution of modern society. Vestigial organs are interesting because the often tells us something of the history of change over time. Whales with stumps of legs, horses with extra toes, ostriches with useless wings, are a few examples These are left over from a different time but now have lost their function. In the western world the notion of signing a legally binding contract that commits two people to stay with each other and to love and cherish each other for their lifetime is a carryover from an earlier time when it was essential to the future of the community that such a contract be upheld. It is also important to say that till death do us part most likely would happen sooner rather than later with an average lifespan for most people of 35yrs.

It is very upsetting for most people to consider that marriage as a legally binding contract for life is a very dangerous and unnecessary part of today's society. It is dangerous because it sometimes leads to desperate suffering when a relationship begins to fail. It is unnecessary because the core element of its original meaning, that of taking responsible care for children, should be legislated for separate from the relationship between the parents. Bringing children into the world is an act of enormous significance and responsibility and can be catered for differently. People get upset with me when I discuss this with them. More specifically those getting married for a second or third time are particularly sensitive when I remind them that if you make a vow to someone to spend your life with them, and then break that vow, you learn that you are someone who can make a lifetime vow and then break it. In this situation, I suggest one should avoid making such vows.

Is there then any authentic basis for the notion of marriage in a modern context of longevity, individualism and planned families? The answer has to be yes! But only if we focus on the human need to ritualise and celebrate significant passages or transitions in our lives. Entering into a long term committed and exclusive relationship is a major event in anyone's life, and as such should be marked by celebration and acknowledgement among one's friend's family and community. The marriage ceremony is the event which states to our community that this is the one whom I have chosen, and who has chosen me to pursue the possibility of a lifetime bond of commitment, friendship, support, intimacy and love. That celebration is the only worthwhile meaning that marriage in the modern context should have. The legal coercion intrinsic to a legal contract for a relationship is no longer a valid concept. I don't expect most people to agree with that any time soon! One solution to the legal element implicit and often unspoken in marriage contract is the notion of the prenuptial contract. A prenuptial contract is a legal contract entered into before marriage, so as to protect the parties from the costs likely to incur should they breach the contract of marriage! There is an absurdity in all of this.

This chapter is only a brief sketch of the pitfalls that inhere in modern ways of looking at love and relationship. The challenge in terms of choosing the person who we invite into that profoundly important part of our lives requires awareness of the delusional power of 'being in love'. It in no way denies that such an experience is important and one of life's great joys. But it is what it is. The other aspects require a sense of knowing the kind of person who fits with you: The one who you enjoy waking up with as well as going to bed with. The person who you can have good conversation with, or you can share mutually enjoyable experiences, the person who shares a common vision for life in all its practicalities and challenges. The person you can spend a lifetime getting to know and still not know fully. Jewish philosopher Immanual Levinas tells us about the absolute 'otherness' of the other person. All attempts to clone, or incorporate that individual into your own image, or to simply service your life task by using their resources is both futile and inauthentic.

All relationships go through periods of difficulty and uncertainty. It is often during such periods that the partners, reacting out of disappointment and disillusionment, behave in ways that can do great damage to the relationship, and limit its potential to survive and flourish. A few of the more common errors are, intentionally inflicting pain on the other, infidelity, emotional withdrawal, and shutting down communication.

Inflicting Pain

There is a fiction buried deep in the psyche of most people that you can get your needs met by your partner if you hurt them. This is a left over from the narcissistic period of childhood whereby screaming and protesting as a result of the pain of hunger or cold or loneliness brought the welcome and soothing response of the mother's breast. I was reminded of this rather forcefully when I listened on youtube.com the 'conversation' with between a distraught Mel Gibson and his ex-wife,! It is very instructive to hear, in real life the pain, rage, hurt, frustration and despair all wrapped up together in this exchange. He couldn't have acted the part better. The temptation to hurt the other because of our own insecurity and infantile dependency is great indeed. And it takes a maturity and considered awareness to refuse its seduction. Acceptance of the inability or even unwillingness of a partner to respond to some of your needs is an important part of being a mature adult. All you can do is ask, explain what the effect is on you, and make a time line for change. Then, you have a choice. If your partner cannot be who you need them to be, then you choose to leave, or you stay with dignity and celebrate the other aspects that are good and wholesome. What you cannot do with any authenticity is stay in chronic unhappiness and loss. You do yourself and your partner a great disservice if you do.

Infidelity

Infidelity drives a stake through the heart of a relationship. Some couples survive the aftermath of an affair and a few even consider that it brought an awareness of what they could lose and a wakeup call to nourish and take better care of their relationship. In general, however, affairs damage relationships and for many, they never really recover. It is a truism that in many situations the affair is simply a symptom of the death of the relationship. In these situations, the affair does not destroy the relationship, it simply confirms that the relationship is already over to all intents and purposes. Sometimes the erring partner has already left on an emotional level but for a variety of reasons (some are outlined above) cannot make the final break. It is also true to say that most affairs do not have the quality that they can sustain after the marriage breaks up. In general, affairs are transitional relationships, untested by the reality of ongoing companionship, daily routine, responsibility for children and the like.

Emotional Withdrawal

Another risk area when relationships are going through a difficult period is that of emotional withdrawal. Men are particularly adept and more susceptible to this form of behaviour. In part it occurs in response to disappointment and resentment, in part it is an intentional intent to punish or hurt the other. Emotional withdrawal shuts down intimacy. It communicates to the other that they are no longer trusted. The worst thing to do when this happens is to try to chase down the emotionally withdrawn partner. This will only lead to further withdrawal and in the case where such withdrawal is being used to hurt, it confirms to the one who wants to hurt that it is working. If someone wants to hurt you, then telling them that it is working does not prevent them from continuing, in fact it is more likely to encourage them to continue. Emotional withdrawal is very painful for both parties. The whole significance of the lover relationship, which is to sustain and nourish each other's love, begins to die. A key element in upholding one's intimate relationship is to take responsibility for one's behaviour in that relationship. The temptation to withdraw emotionally when hurt or disappointment is very strong, the consequences are, however, very significant, and if a relationship is to survive and flourish and recover from the hard times then the temptation to withdraw needs to be carefully avoided. Equally, the temptation to harangue, chase, criticise the one who has withdrawn is also damaging.

Shutting down communication

One of the buzz words in relationship counselling and therapy is that of 'communication'. There is great currency in the notion of a couple having a "communication problem" I sometimes meet clients who are in great distress to the point of barely being able to talk to each other. At such times I often find myself discussing the issue of communication. Rather paradoxically I explain that they do not have a communication problem. They are in fact communicating very well. They are communicating to each other how little they have left to say, how disappointed they are with each other and in some cases how much they dislike or even hate each other. Shutting down communication is a very effective way of punishing another. In some therapy circles it is called the violence of silence. Anyone who has been in a relationship with someone who uses the power of silence knows well its toxic power.

The above is a brief description of the more common ways that people can react when a difficult time arrives, as it always will, in a relationship. It is often the reaction to the problem that in fact destroys the fabric of the relationship rather than the issue itself. And if a relationship is worth saving it is crucially important to avoid these pitfalls, and to seek the help of professional counselling early rather than later. I have seen couples in a potentially good relationships arrive for help too late, because the damage done in trying to cope with the period of disillusionment is too great.

An evolved and enlightened relationship is grounded in a mutual harmony between your true self and your core values and the true self and core values of your partner. If your partner/lover does not harmonise with you in these ways, then the relationship lacks essential qualities of soul mates. Some will say that this is very idealistic and unrealistic. To a large extent this is true. If most people are not evolving into self-awareness, are buying into delusional myths about love, are using freedom to trap themselves, have lost themselves to commodity culture and the raft of self-help books that encourage this path, then we can expect the majority to find themselves in difficult and unfulfilling relationships. My role in writing this is not to suggest that authentic relationships are easy or common. They are not. Rather my intention here is to share the possibility with those who are interested in progressing along a path to an authentic and meaningful life in all its dimensions, including the dimension of intimate love.

Summary

This chapter explored the area of relationships. It advises against the confusion of the 'being in love' experience with that of loving relationship. It also grounds authentic relationships that enhance spiritual growth in a compatibility of values, enjoyment and mutual affirmation. A sexual love relationship adds the dimensions of sexual desire and fidelity. In order to achieve such a relationship, you must already be on the path of your own spiritual growth and have some awareness of who you truly are and what your life task is about. It counsels against using many of the common and destructive reactions when difficult times arrive. And you must avoid people who are damaging or destructive to your emotional health. Only then can you decide who to invite into the role of travelling alongside you through life.

Chapter 6.
Reflective Living.

The Unexamined Life Is Not Worth Living
Socrates

Introduction

Over the last few decades there has been a tremendous rise in interest in meditation as part of a healthy life. One of the more popular methods being what is called transcendental meditation, a method imported into the West by the Maharishi Mahesh Yogi. This approach is grounded in Hindu religious practice and is focused on clearing the mind of all the chatter and distraction by way of breathing exercise and repeating a mantra. A more recent rendition is that of Mindfulness meditation which utilises the same techniques without the need for a quasi-religious mantra. This method and those like it are all forms of what can be called the Eastern mystical tradition. They have some merits as means of stress reduction and sometimes allow for more mental space in the busy minds of frantic people. They also can have a down side in that they can lead to problems with motivation and reduced coping skills for tackling important practical problems in living.

This chapter will introduce a different form of meditation, one that is closer to the Western tradition of using the mind to gain a better understanding of an issue, and discover more creative ways to proceed. In this context the word meditation is a form of focused awareness on a particular subject. This is in this sense that Descartes and others used meditation as a means of gaining philosophical insight.

The Examined Life

One great phrase by Socrates in his challenge to the court in Athens remains as relevant today as it did then: "The unexamined life is not worth living". The following exercises are given with this principle in mind. They too can have the result of a certain pain and distress because they are designed to challenge, provoke and encourage towards authentic living. Thankfully, I do not live in a world where my life is at risk for promoting such things. As you reflect on these exercises you might keep in mind that one of the functions of effective counselling and therapy is to help you in the task of self-knowledge and self-awareness and in that regard, you could enlist the help of a counsellor or spiritual guide as you proceed.

Uniqueness Meditation

First, a story related by Francis Stroud in the introduction to Anthony De Mello's book "Awareness".

A man found an eagle's egg and put it in the nest of a barnyard hen. The eagle hatched with the brood of chicks and grew up with them.

All his life the eagle did what the barnyard chicks did, thinking he was a barnyard chicken. He scratched the earth for worms and insects. He clucked and he cackle. And he would thrash his wings and fly a few feet into the air.

Years passed and the eagle grew very old. One day he saw a magnificent bird above him in the cloudless sky. It glided in graceful majesty among the powerful wind currents with scarcely a beat of its strong golden wings. The old eagle looked up in awe. "Who's that?" He asked.

"That's the eagle, the king of the birds." said his neighbour. We belong to the earth—we're chickens" So the eagle lived and died a chicken, for that's what he thought he was.

Before commenting on the meaning of this story I should counsel again against the notion that we are all eagles in the world of chickens. I dread to think of what would have happened had the farmer put the chicken's egg in the nest of the eagle! If it survived, I can't imagine it trying to catch a rat for his dinner! No, this story is inspirational for another reason. It tells us, in story form, that we can easily live out a life that is a simple copy or imitation of those around us. And in doing, so we can disown important aspects of our unique identity, or never develop our true self. Rather we develop the constructed self-discussed in the earlier chapter. Beneath the constructed self lies the authentic self.

The following exercise may help you to get a clearer picture of that self.

It is important to take some time and space to do the following exercises. Try to set a meditative mood in a quiet room. Soft lighting and gentle music can help to set an atmosphere of calm reflection. A notepad and pencil will also help you to jot down some of the thoughts that occur as you meditate on the following.

Close your eyes and focus on your breathing. Breathe in slowly to the count of 4, hold your breath briefly and breathe out slowly to the count of four. Do this for 4 to 5 minutes. Now imagine that you are watching a video of your life story. Rewind to a time when you felt in harmony with yourself and the world. Now focus your attention on that memory. Imagine that it is playing out in front of you. What was happening in this scene? Write down some key words. What activity were you engaged in? Who was around, if anyone? What was it that made the experience good for you? When you complete this exercise try to discover what this event tells you about yourself. You need to do this exercise several times, each time focusing on a different memory. Gradually a picture will emerge where you will find common themes that tell you about your true self. You may for example find that the memories have a theme of loving care for others, or perhaps a creative task completed. Then again you may have succeeded in some task that you are proud of. Inside these memories are hints of how you want to be in the world.

Another series of exercises focus you on times when you felt 'out of synch'. Remember times when you felt disconnected, distressed and uncomfortable. What was happening? I'm not referring here to events where you were traumatised or frightened. Rather this refers to times you put yourself in a situation where you were functioning well but unhappy with where you had landed. What were you doing, what was going on? Write down what it was that you were unhappy with. As you reflect on the result of these reflections some themes may emerge. You may discover that feeling in harmony with yourself means engaging in certain kinds of self-expression. On the other hand, you may also discover that certain situations leave you feeling at odds with yourself. You may have disowned parts of your true self as you grew into the tasks and responsibilities of adulthood. The challenge facing you is to reclaim these. To do so you must engage in becoming more empowered for change.

Freedom and Empowerment Meditation

An important area of reflection on freedom concerns the way you choose to use your resources. Your most essential resources are your emotional/physical energy, your intellectual/practical skills, your money and your time. We have seen earlier that people can spend their resources in ways that reduce their sense of control and power in life. The simplest example here is in relation to money. The proper functioning of the banking system is to provide financial resources for people to invest in projects that will create better opportunities for themselves, and to allow people to purchase their homes. More recently however the focus of banking is designed to enslave people so that the bank will have a long term claim on their financial resources. Credit card companies, in particular, work on the basis that many people will become so indebted that even by the end of their lives they will still be paying interest on money sometimes borrowed decades earlier. The indirect effect is that their productive energies are a hostage to their debt, and their freedom to make changes is deeply compromised. The same principal applies however in entrapped relationships, and in being owned by one's employer.

Getting free in these areas means taking a close look at how to change the way resources are being spent. Wasting enormous energies in toxic relationships can suck your life dry. Becoming a slave to the opinions of others is another form of disempowerment. If you invest your energies in these ways you will not have any left for your own life.

Take time to focus your attention to the way that you have used your power of choice. As you replay your life story in your imagination, focus on some key decisive moments. Look at the choices you have made and examine them in terms of those that have helped your life to advance, and those that have hindered you. Take each decision and explore the reason why you chose certain paths. What were the strong influences that guided your path? As you reflect on this you will most likely notice that there are patterns in the way that you make decisions. Some of the more common ones concern the influence that others can have on you. Some decisions are made out of fear of rejection or social disapproval. Others are made on impulse without giving serious thought to them. Then others may be based on not respecting or valuing your resources/achievements. Go through each decision carefully and examine to what extent you were actually in charge, or to what extent you were being driven by fear, ignorance, misplaced optimism. Try to notice the difference between good decisions and bad decisions. Make a list of the factors that led to bad ones, and another list that led to good ones. This list will serve you as a guide for how to make better decisions. You will have a clearer understanding of the pitfalls that you are inclined towards, as well as considerations that you need to take into account in going forward

Life Purpose Meditation.

Imagine that you are now eighty-five years old, in good health but a bit feeble. You go for a stroll by the river bank. It is a warm day and the birds are singing. You reach an old cottage where you know there is something good within. As you draw closer you are met by a gentle old lady who invites you inside. As you sit there she congratulates you on a well lived life as she carries a little treasure chest to the table. She explains that all the important parts of that life have been recorded in this treasure chest. She tells you that she is going to leave you with it. She gets up and leaves. You open the lid and therein lies a series of photographs, letters and other artefacts. You take each one and reflect on it. It shows a picture or a symbolic representation of you expressing what is now a cherished memory in your life. Write down what you see. Go through the imagined photos/letters/symbols one by one in your mind's eye until you have a list of what has added up to your good and fulfilled life. This is the future you want to make for yourself, because it is the past you want to remember when you are old.

Relationship Meditation

Because of our exposure to a constant barrage of romantic images in songs, books and films we are not in short supply of imagery connected with romantic love. Thus, the focus on this exercise is more mundane and less exciting. Before embarking on this meditation there are a few important considerations to take into account in addition to what has been written in the previous chapter. First it is important to realise that when we talk of a relationship, we are more accurately talking about how we relate to a particular person. It is a feature of a lot of relationship psychology to lose sight of this fact. Feminist writer Susan Kappeller gives a useful insight into this problem. She writes; *"Although another person is a necessary prerequisite for a relationship, that person is often its principle impediment, the obstacle in our way of making it a happy relationship and realising its potential. If only the other were as we imagine them in our dreams, if only the other conformed to our happiest fantasies, if only the other were truly an object which does not periodically fall out of its role, then our happiness would be complete, and the relationship would no longer be a problem...for we—my relationship and I would be having a perfect partnership...it is the same partnership by the way which I always wanted to have with my mother but which never succeeded because of her !!!"* (p.111).

It is a summer evening and you imagine you are sitting quietly in the company of your beloved. Focus on the attributes that he/she has that attract you and nourish your soul. Write these down. Then focus on a relationship which failed or which caused you much distress and unhappiness. Write down the features that disturbed you. As you do this you will begin to find that there are certain essential attributes which are key to being happy with someone. Additionally, there are certain characteristics that cause you pain and distress. As you continue with this meditation you will get a clearer picture of the kind of person you want to be with. All relationships require some compromise. It is essential to distinguish those things that you can compromise on from those that by doing so you diminish your life. If you discover, through this reflection, that your current relationship is wrong for you, then you are faced with the challenge to do something about this. It may mean getting help to alleviate the difficulties or even support to leave the relationship.

Whatever you do, do not engage in the belief that you can change another person. This is the greatest but unfortunately common source of so much distress in relationships. The person you engage with will not change significantly, and certainly will not change simply because you wish it. They have a right to be themselves in this world and are not to be used as an object for your manipulation. The path to chronic unhappiness is often strewn with naive optimism and a delusional belief that we can change other people into what we want them to be.

Eternal Recurrence Meditation

Many people want to live forever because they believe that it will take forever to learn how to live. The following meditation is useful in helping locate the aspects of lived experience that we want to have in our lives and to recognise those we want to change or avoid. I have taken it verbatim from philosopher Friedrich Nietzsche. *"What, if some day or night a demon were to steal after you into your loneliest loneliness and say to you 'This life as you now live it and have lived it, you will have to live once more and innumerable times more, and there will be nothing new in it, but every pain and every joy and every thought and sigh, and everything unutterably small or great in your life will have to return to you"* (p.273).

Take time to reflect on those aspects of your life that you could say to: Yes, I would want these to recur. And then turn your thoughts to what you do not want to experience if it were to be given to you again. This is a powerful exercise, and in some situations, there will be events that have happened of which you had no part in creating, and over which now you have no control. There will be, however, significant parts of your life that you can still work on towards change. As you write down the details that emerge from this exercise, you can explore the resources, support and time you may need to make these changes

Summary

These exercises will give you important information on your true self, your way of using choice and the paths you need to take. With this information the 'now' becomes incredibly pivotal and you can begin to make conscious and informed choices about your life. These gems of self-understanding become a beacon to you. Yes, there will be times when you will go off course, but you will not stray for long because you now have a navigation guide for your life. Living in the now also becomes so much more meaning filled and fulfilling. While the exercises above use the past and the future as reference points, they are only that. They help you to create a 'now' that is right for you. You can then enjoy the present for itself, and also because you know it is going to become a good past. We cannot change the past we have right now, but we can change the past we are going to have tomorrow.

Afterword.

Thank you for taking time to read this book. I hope it has been of value to you. I understand that it is not always easily digested and is written in a very condensed manner. I am also aware of some of its limitations. I am sure there are flaws that will come to my attention through the critique of others. One such limitation is that it is strongly focused on what can be called individualism. Individualism places most emphasis on the person as being responsible for who they become. There are several issues that powerfully affect personal freedom that are not explored in depth in this book.

The power of social, economic and cultural forces in moulding and containing what a person can become has been discussed only in a limited way. I have tried to show that while these considerations are important there is always a modicum of freedom available to us. This topic is explored in more detail in a different book of mine "Misled? How Ideology Captures your Mind".

I have not dwelt at any length on the power of unconscious forces that determine some of our choices. I believe that living an aware life is a lifelong project. Once you begin to live reflectively, the power of the unconscious lessens. Freud understood that the great value of therapy is in making the unconscious conscious through a therapeutic dialogue. I believe that reflection and meditation can also go some way towards that goal.

I have referred only briefly to the impact of trauma, particularly those life damaging psychic wounds inflicted by abuse in the formative years of childhood. These can have seriously debilitating consequences on how the 'now' is experienced. They can also cause paralysing effects when a traumatised person tries to change direction. I have written elsewhere on this topic and would refer the reader to that work. (Healing the Hurts of Childhood)

I have not mentioned addiction. It is perhaps the most enslaving of conditions. Again, this is the topic of a different work to which the reader can refer if appropriate. (Understanding Addiction: A Guide to Recovery)

Other crucial areas that are related to the way we choose to be in the world are the ways that we develop morality, ethics and beliefs about right and wrong. The problem of evil is not discussed in the level of depth required to do it justice. My book "The Path to Mass Evil" examines one important dimension of the problem. The claims of truth in religion are another important topic in terms of what people believe and how they live. These and other areas are for another time.

Some people see these forces as far too powerful than those an individual can marshal for themselves. And, in some instances they may be right. This book does not venture there, rather it is an aspirational work that encourages people to use whatever freedom they have to expand that freedom and to create more authentic lives for themselves. If enough people do that, we just may see some change towards a more authentic world.

Michael Hardiman

June 2023

References

Baudrillard. J. Simulacra and Simulation. 1994. Michigan University Press. 1994

Beck. U. Risk Society. Toward a new Modernity. Cambridge. Polity. 1992. P.165

Browning. C. Ordinary Men. Reserve Police Battalion and the Final Solution in Poland. Harper Collins 1992

Becker. E. Escape from Evil. New York. The Free Press 1975
Byrne. R. The Secret. New York. Atria Books 2006

De. Mello. A. Awareness. London. Fount. 1997

Descartes. R. Meditations. In: Routledge philosophy guidebook to Descartes and the meditations. New York, Routledge.

Fisk. R. The Great War for Civilisation. The Conquest of the Middle East. London. Harper Perennial. 2006

Foucault M. The Archaeology of Knowledge (trans A. Sheridan). New York. Pantheon.1972

Hardiman. M Children Under the Influence. Cork. Paragon. 1993
Hardiman. M. Healing the Hurts of Childhood. Dublin, Newleaf. 1998

Hardiman. M. Understanding Addiction: A Guide to Recovery New York. Random House.2000

Hardiman. M. The Path to Mass Evil. Routledge. New York. 2023.

Hardiman. M Misled? How Ideology Captures Your Mind. Paragon. Galway 2024

Heidegger. M. Being and Time Oxford. Basil Blackwell 1967

Hobbes. T. Leviathan. In: From Plato to Derrida. 4th ed. New Jersey. Prentice Hall 2003

Kappeller. S. The Will to Violence: The politics of personal behaviour. Cambridge. The Polity Press. 1995

Kierkegaard.S The Concept of Dread. 1844 ed. Trans:.Walter Lowrie. (Princeton University Press). 1957

Lewis. C.S Mere Christianity. Glasgow. Fount. !978 Maslow. A. Motivation and Personality. New York Harper and Row. 1970

Milgram, S. Obedience to Authority; An Experimental View. Harper Collins 1974
Myss. C. Why People Don't Heal and How They Can. London. Bantham, 1997.
Nietzsche. F. The Gay Science. New York. Vintage Books. 1974
Nietzsche. F. Thus Spake Zarathustra. Harmondsworth Penguin. 1961
Nietzsche. F. The Genealogy of Morals. New York. Vintage. 1973.
O'Sullivan. K. Poor. London. Penguin. 2023

Pascal. B. Pensees.b267/k188 In: From Plato to Derrida. 4th ed. New Jersey. Prentice Hall.

Peck. S. The Road Less Travelled. London, Rider. 1982

Rand. A. Atlas Shrugged. London. Penguin. 1999

Ross. C. Pseudoscience in Biological Psychiatry. New York. Wiley & Sons. 1978

Rousseau. J,J. The Social Contract. Book One. In: Rousseau Selections. Ed Martin Cranston New York. Macmillan. 1988

Russell. B. History of Western Philosophy London, Routledge 1996 p.631.

Sartre. J.P. The Psychology of Imagination. (trans B.Frechtman), New York. Washington Square Press. 1966.

Schopenhauer. A The World as Will and Representation Trans. By E.F.J..Payne. Dover. 1966

Socrates. In: The Last Days of Socrates. Plato. London Penguin. 2003

Warren. R. The Purpose Driven Life. Michigan Zondervan 1993

Weintraub. The Value of the Individual. Chicago University Press. 1978p.xii-xiii

Wiesal. E. Cited in: Peace Love and Healing. Bernie Siegal. London. Arrow. p.280 1990

Zimbardo. P. In: Haney, C., Banks, W.C. & Zimbardo, P.G. (1973) A study of prisoners and guards in a simulated prison. Naval Research Review, 30, 4-17.